Difficult Questions Kids Ask— and Are Too Afraid to Ask—About Divorce

*Meg F. Schneider
and Joan Zuckerberg, Ph.D.*

Consulting Editor: Amalia Lee, Ph.D.

a fireside book
published by Simon & Schuster

FIRESIDE
Rockefeller Center
1230 Avenue of the Americas
New York, NY 10020

FIRESIDE and colophon are registered
trademarks of Simon & Schuster Inc.

Designed by Elina D. Nudelman

Manufactured in the United States of America

1   3   5   7   9   10   8   6   4   2

Library of Congress Cataloging-in-Publication Data
Schneider, Meg F.
Difficult questions kids ask—and are too afraid to ask—about
divorce
Meg Schneider & Joan Zuckerberg
consulting editor Amalia Lee.
p.   cm.
1. Children of divorced parents. 2. Divorce—Psychological
aspects. I Offerman-Zuckerberg, Joan. II Title.
HQ777.5.S36 1996   96-20152
306.89—dc20   CIP

ISBN 0-684-81436-6

ACKNOWLEDGMENTS

I want to thank the many parents who allowed me, with generosity and honesty, to look at a most painful time in their lives. I am indebted to my mother, Sally Schneider, for seeing me through my own difficulties, and reminding me, always, that what I do counts. And of course I would like to thank my editor, Betsy Radin, for her encouragement, suggestions and integrity. This is the book I wanted to write, and she along with the ever insightful Dr. Joan Zuckerberg helped me get there. Dr. Amalia Lee's commitment was a true gift.

MFS

The idea for this book came from a personal source, as most creative journeys do. I thank Meg Schneider, my coauthor, for inviting me to embark with her on this journey, and her ability to translate complex psychological concepts into lively, down-to-earth, accessible language. If this book can facilitate better communication between parent and child during a particularly painful time, then our objective will have been met. Thank you to Dr. Leanne Domash, who in the beginning stage supplied critical information about her experiences as a coauthor. Thank you to the parents and children I have treated over the years who, in their courageous struggle to make things right, inspired me to continue to hang in there despite the inevitable swings in analytic work. Thank you to my sons, Joshua and Benjamin, who in their search for truth and clarity keep me honest. Finally, thank you to my beloved husband and friend, Richard Zuckerberg, whose belief in me keeps me going. I dedicate this book to him.

—JZ

To my boys.

May you never stop asking questions.

MFS

CONTENTS

Introduction:

Open Dialogues Heal

Sally, a lively seven-year-old, came with her worried parents to my office for her initial appointment. The family was at the beginning stages of the divorce process and was here because Sally's parents had, in an earlier meeting, expressed concern about their daughter.

Sally, who had always been a cheerful and outgoing child, had suddenly become fearful of many things. Dogs, visiting a friend on her own or simply being upstairs while her parents were downstairs seemed cause for alarm. Sally seemed unhappy much of the time and was having difficulty getting along with the other children in her class. She was also having nightmares, after which it was difficult to settle her down. "We've told her that we will always love her and there is nothing to be scared about," her parents had assured me. "What else is there to say? She's so young. What could she understand? She doesn't seem all that interested in talking about the divorce anyway. We bring it up sometimes, but she turns us off."

Sally followed me into my office, though somewhat reluctantly. That day, and for a few sessions thereafter, she promptly "got into gear" and proceeded to act in a charming, free-spirited manner. She told jokes, laughed easily, moved from chair to chair pretending to be me, then a clown, then a teacher, all the while telling me charming little stories. During her third visit, after I felt she'd gotten the message that this was definitely "her time," I pulled out some paper and crayons and asked if she'd like to draw something—anything. She could show it to other people or we could keep it just here, in my office.

As she began to draw I talked about why her parents had brought her to my office. I mentioned her dreams and the struggles she'd been having with her friends, and told her I thought maybe I could help. Anything she told me would be just between us. Sally began to describe her nightmares easily enough. "There's a monster," she said, "and it keeps waiting by my bed and telling me it's going to swallow me right up. I call my daddy but he doesn't hear me. Also my mommy. But they don't come. I don't know why. . . ."

She looked down at the paper and busily began drawing. Moments later it was covered with vessels. Rowboats. Canoes. They seemed to be in a vast and rough ocean, and each held a small figure of a little girl clutching a doll.

"It looks to me like you want to go somewhere," I said. "Someplace gentle and safe. You know, Sally, you could think of yourself that way here."

Sally seemed to mull that over for a long moment. And then she replied, with great relief, "You mean I can be me?"

It was such a moving question, heartfelt and coming from someplace very deep.

I leaned forward and said, "Yes. You can. Who are you?"

Sally, it turned out, was a little girl caught in the clutches of a terrible fear. Or, I should say, the terrible unknown.

She knew her parents were getting divorced. She understood they would no longer all be living together. She even seemed to believe that they loved her very much. She knew what might be termed the "nuts and bolts" of what was happening.

But what she didn't know or understand was, to put it simply . . . everything else.

She was afraid of why it had happened. Had she done something? She was confused about where she'd sleep and with whom and when. She was angry, but afraid to be. Sad, but fighting it. Resentful, but not clear why. Sally knew she was loved, but she wasn't sure what that meant. After all, wasn't everyone leaving her? Dividing her? Everything felt horrible, but everyone was saying it wasn't so bad. She saw things one way, but it seemed she was supposed to see them another. This was terrifying. What was the truth? Whom could she trust?

So Sally wanted to climb into a canoe, surrounded by water, and find a better place.

"But we've been open with her," Sally's mother insisted. "Still, she's just a little girl. We don't have all the answers ourselves. How much could we tell her?"

The answer to that question is the reason my coauthor and I wrote this book.

You need to tell your child everything she needs to know, whether she is able to articulate what that is or not. And if you yourself don't know, you need to say that. Because it is the truth. Anything short of this is a kind of "conspiracy of silence."

We want to be able to help parents tell the truth in a way that will inform rather than frighten, strengthen rather than weaken, and build trust rather than visit betrayal.

To make this happen, parents need to do two things. One, create an emotional environment that allows for conversation—that communicates their willingness to discuss difficult details. And two, respect their child's instincts and deep "knowing."

A divorce is an upsetting and difficult event. To try to present it as a problem of limited scope or emotional import is to deny the value of the family life you have shared to date. It is also an insult to the ability and courage of your child to perceive the magnitude of the event.

As it turned out, Sally's parents, in an effort to protect their daughter from pain, had held back way too much information. But this was not just an act of parental protectiveness. After a number of sessions, they came to realize they were also trying to spare themselves. The pain of seeing her hurt, and the fear of facing what the divorce would cause in their own lives, had rendered them silent.

They had failed to respect their daughter's ability to "know," in a nonverbal way, that something huge was happening, and her need for help in bringing her thoughts and fears out into the light of day.

A divorce does not have to be traumatic. But it can be so, if parents and children fail to communicate.

●

This book will give you, the parents, a sense of how to talk about what's happened and what's going to happen and how children really feel both on the surface and deep below, where so many fears fester. It will help you bring their feelings out into the open.

The following pages contain information and suggestions on talking about the sense of blame, or being deserted, or feeling torn or betrayed, or wanting a reconciliation, so that the feelings and fantasies become more tolerable.

This book explores the apparent as well as hidden questions that haunt children as they try to weather the confusing, frightening and painful aspects of a divorce. Here you will find the insights, skills and words—in short, the tools—to start and maintain an open communication about divorce with your child.

The questions in this book were drawn from my twenty-five years of professional experience working with families and children in crisis, as well as from my coauthor's own personal experience with divorce and those of the people she interviewed. These questions come from the heart. Some will seem more general, others more idiosyncratic, the way children can be. They may speak of a fear that seems to encompass everything, or one that seems related to just one tiny event. The key is to answer what's literally being asked as well as what's lurking beneath the surface. The hidden questions spring from my professional experience and intuitive sense of what is really going on, based on the work I have done with young patients and their parents struggling with divorce. And they are also a reflection of what children have eventually voiced when led to a comfortable place where they feel it's safe to ask. (Generally this happens once you've supplied most of the answers!)

These hidden questions cut to the heart of the matter. They deal with issues which are too embarrassing or frightening or guilt-provoking to even acknowledge, no less put into words.

But these are the questions that need answers most.

We have constructed, then, suggested answers that cover not only the apparent questions but the ones that are rarely expressed as well. Whatever we have missed, whatever curveball your child sends your way, there is enough territory covered here to put together an answer that will go a long way towards helping your child.

Sally had appeared in my office because she hadn't been given the "go ahead," or the right to ask questions. She'd been coaxed into silence by two caring, well-meaning, but frightened parents.

As Sally began to express herself, and her parents grew more comfortable and able to address first their own feelings and then hers, her nightmares and fears began to subside.

It was a slow process. As it will be for you. Not every fear can be faced at once. Not every situation can be resolved as quickly as you would like. Not every child will be as able as the next to ask for what she needs.

This divorce process is something you and your child need to feel your way through.

But "feel" is the key. You need to allow for all of your child's feelings. You need to communicate that her fears shouldn't be hidden away. That her anger and confusion should be expressed. That her sadness is her right and not something from which she needs to protect herself or you.

Because in the end, it's not the feeling that will hurt your child. It's her lack of awareness, or denial of it, that can lead to the long-term problems associated with divorce.

Divorce needn't be a tragedy. You as a parent have the power to make it not just a door that closes, but one that opens.

And the place to begin is through conversations that embrace the painful truths. Your child can take it.

We hope this book will help you do the same.

Joan Zuckerberg, Ph.D.

Part I

Making Questions Possible

1.

There's No Such Thing as a Simple Question

- How come Daddy is living with someone else now?
- Why do we have to move? I like my room!
- How come you don't love Mommy anymore?

Divorce is a painful and confusing process for any family.

There is turmoil and ambivalence through every phase. Questions abound, from the decision-making stage to the difficult years of practical and emotional upheaval, through to when the time comes to optimistically explore the future.

Thoughtful adults strive to reach the decision to divorce in a measured and serious fashion. It doesn't always work, of course. Rage and hurt can interfere with clear thinking. And no matter how much time is taken to think things through, and no matter how right the decision might ultimately feel, many adults are still left mired in questions:

Could I have avoided this? What will my life be like now? Did I do something wrong? Will I ever be happy again? What will everyone think? How could this have happened to me?

Unfortunately, children will often harbor the same questions. Only theirs spring not just from reality-based concerns, but also from a wellspring of fantasies, fears and anxieties. Their questions, while sometimes seemingly simple, are often riddled with misunderstandings and hurt (Doesn't Daddy love me anymore?), infused with self-doubt and guilt (Did it happen because I threw my toys on the floor?) or designed to hide feelings of intense anger and crushing disappointment (So, are we still going to go on that canoe trip?). Sadly, many of these questions are answered by parents in a perfunctory manner. Only the apparent question is addressed, and usually minimally, while the subtext lies buried and ignored.

This is dangerous and hurtful for the child.

A child's capacity to make changes in his life is heightened by a healthy, communicative relationship with both his parents.

If they can share their thoughts, fears and feelings with each other, there will exist a trust and confidence that no divorce process can take away.

It should be stressed that the divorce process is not just the time it takes to sign the papers. It begins with the dark days before the separation and continues through the years after the divorce. Questions do not just disappear after everyone's "gotten used to" the situation. Children, as they grow older and enter different phases of their own lives, will often feel the need to revisit the issues surrounding the divorce. Their understanding will change with age. They will seek to comprehend what has happened in an effort to make healthful commitments and attachments in their own personal lives.

A divorce does not have to be devastating. It does not have to be the defining principle in every family member's life. An unhappy marriage can be far more devastating to the well-being of children than a divorce. While a divorce is painful to everyone, it is important to remember that when the door opens and someone walks out, that same door allows new experiences in.

How your child weathers the pain and anxiety of a divorce will depend as much upon your view of the event as it will on the actual words you use. The undercurrent of your message, the words spoken and unspoken, will speak volumes about what the divorce means and what the future may hold.

A divorce can feel like a terrible secret to a child—as if it is something that is "better left unsaid." The more reluctant you are to speak openly, the more likely it is you will have a child who cannot ask a thing. Or if he can, he might be too frightened to listen with a clear head.

Good communication between you and your child can make all the difference.

Why Children Have Trouble Asking Questions

Children most often have trouble asking questions because they're afraid of what will happen when they do.

They may not be conscious of what they're afraid of, but they have a host of fears nonetheless. What if they are horrified by the answer? What if parents get angry or upset? What if they're told not to be silly or not to feel a particular way?

Who in their right mind would set themselves up for this kind of pain? No one. And so children insist they have no questions, or ask the ones that bear only the slightest resemblance to what they really would like to know.

Further complicating the above is a developmental component, especially in younger children.

CHILDREN CAN ONLY UNDERSTAND WHAT THEIR AGE ALLOWS

There is an established developmental sequence that rules the ability of children to interpret and understand the environment. Children's limited verbal abilities and emotional sophistication make it difficult for them to ask questions that reflect their deepest fears and feelings. They don't have the language, and they also lack the ability to conceptualize certain matters. The stage of a child's neurological and resultant cognitive development can add to the confusion and fear of a divorce, making it difficult for him to ask either the "real question" or even any questions at all.

The concept of time is an excellent illustration of this. A young child, told that he will see Daddy in two days, may not know what that means. He might think it means what we would term an hour, or it may sound as if the visit will take place in another life. His confusion might not only scare him but also render him unwilling to ask for an explanation.

Then there are issues of continuity and constancy. A young child may have little sense of what happens, or what to expect, when things or people disappear. If Daddy leaves the house, is Daddy gone forever? Again, such fears could easily stand in the way of a child's desire to ask a question.

An immature sense of relationships, a reflection of the stages in the development of social awareness, can profoundly confuse a child during this time. He may still be at the point where Timmy is his "best friend" because, for instance, the boy sits next to him in class. Therefore, it might follow that almost any man you meet could be husband number two.

Finally, young children have a distorted sense of cause and effect, which corrects itself over time as life experience gradually clarifies the picture. But just as their social awareness is limited, so do children make connections that are inaccurate. Daddy wouldn't have left, your daughter might think, if only she'd cleaned her room. You could be getting a divorce because Daddy's meeting went on too long. The perception of reality is distorted. The questions are often off base.

It is important to be aware of your young child's neurological and resultant cognitive ability to conceptualize, so that in offering information or answering a muddled question, you are sure your answer is understood. You can always revisit topics in greater depth later.

CHILDREN HAVE TROUBLE ARTICULATING THEIR FEELINGS

Children are not sufficiently self-aware to address what is truly causing them pain. The complicated nature of a divorce, then, can be too much for them to sort out on their own. On the one hand they sense they are loved, and on the other hand they feel as if they are being abandoned. How can these two feelings exist side by side and be understood? And which is more true? The love or the desertion? These are not thoughts children can formulate clearly. They are more apt to ask, "Where is Daddy going this weekend?" than "How come Daddy isn't visiting me tomorrow? Is he ever coming again?"

Children can't articulate their thoughts on divorce because they do not have the vocabulary or emotional sophistication to deal with conflict, and because they are too frightened to think clearly.

CHILDREN ARE TOO FRIGHTENED TO ASK THE MOST PAINFUL QUESTIONS

Children of all ages fear what the answers to their questions might be. They don't want to know if Daddy is never coming back, or if Mommy never loved them, or if they may end up living in those homeless shelters they see on TV, or if Mommy and Daddy are never going to get back together, or if they will ever know who is going to tuck them in at night, or if the sadness they feel is going to be with them forever.

They don't want to know the answers because they fear the worst. To them, for a time at least, divorce is Armageddon. It's bad enough they suspect all is lost. It's another thing altogether to know it's so.

It's a dreadful way to live, but to many children it's better than opening the door and stepping off the face of the earth. Better to stand on the edge and pray real hard that nothing pushes you over. . . .

PARENTS MAY BE RELUCTANT TO LISTEN

Unresolved about their own problems, or overwhelmed with guilt and anxiety, parents may express an unwillingness to face the issues. "You're too young to understand," a mother might reply to a troubled six-year-old who screws up his courage to ask, "But why is Daddy leaving?"

"I don't think we need to discuss that now," might be said to a ten-year-old who is somewhat able to face the confusion and who wants to know, "Are you going to have a boyfriend soon?"

The trouble with this kind of reluctance is that children will often conclude two things. One, that they themselves are unimportant, and two, that it's wrong to want to know.

Parents who are unwilling to help their children understand, no matter what the reason, will leave their children feeling dismissed and belittled. Their feelings, they will conclude, are inconsequential. Their ability to understand, sadly lacking.

Also, upon being told they don't need to know something, children will usually make the leap to thinking they're bad for having asked and that these matters should remain secret. Of course, if these things are secret, it's easy for children to also conclude the answers must be horrible. . . .

WHEN CHILDREN DO ASK QUESTIONS THEIR FEELINGS MAY BE DENIED

Parents who feel guilty about their own role in their children's unhappiness may refute their children's emotions. A tearful "Everything is changing!" might be greeted with, "Don't be silly. Everything is the same. It's just that Daddy is living elsewhere." Filled with regret and a sense of responsibility for this radical change in family life, some parents might seek to deny its effects by pretending it isn't *such* a big deal after all. A divorce is something that happens between husband and wife, they might try to believe; the children don't have to be touched all that much.

Unfortunately, this self-serving approach will confuse and hurt the children terribly. They know that something big has happened. They know it's going to affect the patterns of their lives. They know they're losing something. But here is a trusted adult saying to them, essentially, "What you know isn't so."

This attitude has the destructive effect of both shaking up the children's faith in their own perceptions, and of forcing them to try and trick themselves into believing the "new reality." It won't work. In the end the children's knowledge will emerge in another form. Depression.

CHILDREN FEAR THEIR QUESTIONS WILL HURT OR ANGER THEIR PARENTS

Children are deeply intuitive about their parents' feelings. They can sense when something is making a parent distressed or uncomfortable. Unfortunately, especially for younger children, "distressed" and "uncomfortable" are not easily understood words or feelings. So they may conclude that the parent is simply angry with them. That their questions are annoying. And that if they continue to ask them, the parent will become irritated and leave forever.

If a child is not afraid of angering the parent, he may be afraid of hurting him, or of what will happen if the child doesn't take care of him. "Are you sad?" might get swallowed up and replaced with "Want to read a book?" The child may have seen the parent visibly upset, perhaps even crying. This can be terrifying to a child. If the parent is this upset, then who is in control? Who can make things okay? Is the child supposed to be the adult now? Terrified at the thought that the parent may not be able to stay in charge, the child would rather swallow his questions than find himself the head of the household.

SOME FATHERS ARE NOT PRACTICED IN ADDRESSING CERTAIN PROBLEMS

Though more and more fathers are becoming emotionally available to their children, there are still a great number who are not practiced in the art of having emotionally open conversations with their children. (Mothers too, but we'll get to that issue in the next chapter.)

Fathers have often not been the parent regularly confronted with an upset or angry or confused child. Their communication skills, therefore, can be weak.

"Everything is going to be okay," this parent might insist to an upset child who manages to blurt out, "Why can't you come over more often?" A gift at visiting time may seem, to the father, an expression of love and his wish for the child to feel secure, but to the child it may feel as if he's being asked to take the gift in return for silence.

And so the child obeys. After all, if he asks questions, Daddy might disappear.

Children Find Solace in Magical Thinking

Even in the most intact, loving and constant family, magical thinking persists, particularly in children between the ages of three and eight. This is the belief that if something is wished for hard enough it will be so. In the case of divorce, children simply hope it will go away. (Or, if the tension is bad enough, they may wish for divorce, only to be horrified, most often, if it actually happens.)

They think that if they don't ask questions, if they don't make it more concrete, if they don't hear their parents talking about it openly, perhaps all this talk about Daddy or Mommy moving out will go away. Maybe not immediately. But soon.

Silence is the key.

Hidden questions, hidden trouble.

Or, even better, no questions, no trouble.

It's little wonder children of almost any age have trouble asking questions. The younger the child, the more apt he is to be lost in a mire of fears, unable to identify or articulate his anxiety. He would rather deny. Think magical thoughts.

The slightly older child may be able to articulate his fears to a limited extent, but he will be reluctant to ask questions for fear of what he'll hear and how it will make others feel. Fearing abandonment, he may conclude it's best to just act "good." Or, unable to cope with feelings of sadness or loss, this child may allow himself to feel only anger. He'll strike out rather than ask a meaningful question.

The even older child may simply be too upset to want to express anything at all. He'd rather push it away. The disappointment is too great. The realities, too unhappy to focus on. His anger may burst forth in fits or turn inward. Teenagers are notorious for endangering themselves because of how threatened they feel inside. Acting out can become severe.

Your Child's Fears, Whether You Are Married or Divorced

Your child's inability to articulate questions about divorce becomes especially understandable when you consider the emotional underpinnings of his life, even in the best of circumstances.

Children who are trying to cope with a threatened marriage are burdened with, and sometimes buried by, a difficult set of fears which even children of a functional family must wrestle with on a daily basis. The difference is that the children from the intact home (provided it is a well-functioning one!) can consistently comfort themselves with evidence that their fears are not seeing the light of day. Children from a home which is experiencing a disruption in the marital relationship see their worst fears coming to life.

These most basic childhood fears relate to the unknown, to issues of safety, to a definition of the self and to the need for protection. In the children of a divorced home, these fears can take on a new and ominous meaning and could have a permanent impact on issues of trust, commitment and the ability to sustain a long-term relationship. Fears of betrayal and abandonment can haunt people throughout their lives.

Children must get help to sort out what's real and what's not and to see how the divorce is clouding their vision. What they find out will be an incredible relief. A chance to neutralize the monster in the closet. An opportunity to put things in perspective. A way of seeing the problem as outside of themselves instead of something they have wrought and must therefore be consumed by.

The classic childhood fears during a divorce are almost like having a nightmare and waking up to find it real.

What follow are the most common "divorce" fears, which are, in fact, more intense forms of fears that all children experience no matter what's happening in their family.

"I'M AFRAID OF BEING ALONE" BECOMES, IN A DIVORCE, "I'M BEING LEFT ALONE"

The role of attachment between parent and child is central to normal development. Infants, two hours old, can recognize their mother's smell. As early as two months old, if not sooner, they may be making communicative eye contact with their mother and can readily distinguish the human face from other sights. By the age of six to nine months, their smile becomes quite selective. Their attachment to the mother deepens and the children start differentiating between caregivers. Research has found that the more easily babies receive warmth and quick attention to their needs, the smoother the transition to the next developmental stage. A foundation is set.

As toddlers, children use their most familiar others as the base from which to venture out into the world. If the bonds are strong, if the children believe that the parent is not going anywhere, the easier they go about their job of getting out there and exploring.

It is these early attachments which lay the groundwork for children's capacity to feel empathy, compassion and love. Even more critically, it is from these attachments that they form a fundamental sense of whether they are lovable and can trust others. Secure bonds are a wonderful gift, allowing children to confidently move outward knowing that home base is always there.

To achieve the confidence these bonds foster, children must be sure of their ability to get their parents' attention and love when they need it. When children can't count on this sort of relationship an anxiety results, which may impact their ability to trust in any significant others later on.

WHY DIVORCE ADDS TO THE PROBLEM

In a divorce, one parent leaves. For a young child, in particular a three- to ten-year-old, this can be perceived as the worst nightmare come true. What will happen to her now? Whom can she go to with her problems? Will the other parent stay or will he or she leave as well? If so, what will happen? When will he or she be back? Who will feed her, hug her, make play dates, tuck her in at night? And, most essentially, to whom does she belong?

Anxieties abound, intensifying every time the remaining parent simply goes out for an evening. Bedtime rituals can become endless, and parental tempers can grow very short.

It's little wonder, in this atmosphere, that children are unable to begin formulating the questions that plague them most. Who would want to be told, if they fear they are being deserted, "Yes, the center of your life is no longer available to you"?

It's bad enough to fear something. It's even worse to receive validation of that fear.

"I HOPE THE BAD GUYS GO AWAY" BECOMES, IN A DIVORCE, "THE BAD GUYS ARE GOING TO GET ME"

All children struggle with the conflict between wanting autonomy and wanting to feel protected. The younger child, between the ages of about two and four, begins to imagine the classic array of fears in response to this dilemma. Hungry, fanged animals lurk under the rocking chair, wicked trolls tap on the window, witches on brooms levitate in wait and masked robbers skulk around every corner. The child is angry at his parents because he feels dependent upon them, but is afraid to express his anger because he needs them so much. Instead, he allows himself to be both angry at and fearful of these creatures, and by allowing his parents to comfort him, he experiences their love with less conflict.

The older child, however, may act out due to the internal conflict of vulnerability vs. autonomy. A "silence" of anger and resentment may develop. He may argue with your rules, all the while being somewhat grateful for them. Grades may drop. Or because of his confusion and conflict, drugs may be an enticement, as he tries to sort out his strengths from his vulnerabilities, his need for independence from his need for parental love.

WHY DIVORCE ADDS TO THE PROBLEM

In a divorce, the young child's fears may grow more intense because his anger at actually being left is so great. Afraid to be furious at the parent who seems to be deserting him, or the one he now fears will also disappear, the amount of emotion he invests in the "bad guys" is bound to grow.

For the slightly older child, the loss of protection becomes a bit more literal. He may worry that robbers will break in. What will happen if there's a fire? With only one parent but two children in the house, who will help whom? There is an unconscious contract in the child's mind that his parent is there to protect him from all evil forces. If a parent physically removes himself from the home, the child will be left feeling frightened and exposed.

Such a response can place parents in a dilemma. They may want to comfort, but too much coddling of an older child can cause him to regress, leading to a myriad of other problems.

"IF I DO SOMETHING BAD WILL YOU STILL LOVE ME?" BECOMES, IN A DIVORCE, "DID I SEND MOMMY/DADDY AWAY?"

As babies grow older, their awareness of sexual pleasure (received from such simple things as washing or diapering) and parental love evolve into a kind of romantic love for their parents. Sometimes this is true of just the opposite sex parent but very often it is true of both. Their love finds expression through their physicality and words. The boy may constantly reach out for his mother's breasts, remembering, somewhere in his mind, the nursing experience, and repeatedly ask if he can sleep next to her at night. The girl may want to snuggle in her daddy's lap for hours on end or be totally amorous and admiring of her mother, wanting to be just like her at every turn.

Children do not always experience these feelings conflict-free. While they may enjoy them greatly, inside there might be a pretty hefty dose of guilt and fear. Sometimes the feeling of romantic love for the opposite sex parent, for instance, is displayed in a hostile way towards the parent with whom the child feels in competition. A boy might suggest to his father that he go away for a trip. A girl might venomously snap at her mother that Daddy "loves me best."

This is all completely natural, and something each parent should try and take in their stride. The competitive and passionate energy your child throws out is a natural part of her development. But something else is going on too. Your child is coming to understand that there is a special relationship between her two parents. A sexual one that she cannot share in. This is a healthy realization and one that will help her in her continuing quest to separate from you. As she reaches adolescence her own more appropriate romantic relationships will take center stage. There will be a reinvestment of love and affection from parent to peer.

WHY DIVORCE ADDS TO THE PROBLEM

When parents separate, and one parent leaves, the child who has romantic feelings for one parent can come to believe that his feeling of anger or competitiveness with the missing parent actually drove him out. That somehow he's won. He has stolen the heart of the loved one.

But of course it's a Pyrrhic victory. He may have won his mother but he's driven away his protector, his role model, his adored other parent. Not to mention the fact that his love for his mother has in the past been safely contained by the knowledge that his father stands in the way. If this father steps aside the child can feel terrified. He knows that the role he has sometimes desired is too much for him. He is not a man yet. Having achieved his dream, he can begin to feel frightened and overwhelmed.

Also, convinced he is responsible for the family's breakup, he may become profoundly guilty, sad and ultimately depressed. His deepest secrets, he may think, have brought on the calamity. He may even believe himself to be wicked. Or all-powerful.

◗

Finally, there is a fear that for the most part does not impact heavily a child living in an intact, healthy family. It's a fear that intensifies sharply in response to a divorce and is driven largely by the egocentric nature of the child and his normal, nagging self-doubt. And that fear is of *rejection.* I am not *worth* staying around for. I am not *good enough* to keep them together. "Someone else" is better.

"I WISH I WERE SMARTER, PRETTIER, FASTER" BECOMES, IN A DIVORCE, "I'M NOT GOOD ENOUGH TO MAKE YOU STAY"

Children of any age feel rejected when a parent leaves. To them the mother is not just leaving the father but leaving the children as well. It is extremely difficult for them to draw the line and recognize the difference. Children identify more with the parent who is being left (the victim), since that is the role closest to their own inner experience. They may feel "ditched" along with the adult if indeed that is the way he or she is feeling. Adolescents are capable of some finer discriminations on this point, but even they are apt to feel more in common with the parent left behind.

Unfortunately children also try to come up with an explanation for the desertion and, most often, it takes the form of self-criticism. "If only I were prettier," the girl might think. "If he'd been prouder of me," the boy might conclude. It is extremely difficult for children, no matter what the age—because of their egocentrism, need to be loved and approved of, and desire to be one or both parents' only love—to say, "This has to do with the two of them. I'm out of it."

To the children, they too are being left behind. There must be a reason. They must be to blame. They must not measure up.

They must try to be better. . . .

●

The above classic fears—fears of the self, abandonment, helplessness and developing sexuality—are exacerbated by divorce.

But *egocentrism,* a basic characteristic of childhood thinking we've just touched on, is behind all the fears just discussed, which make children afraid to question too closely.

Simply put, this condition of childhood leaves children feeling that the sun rises because they get up in the morning and sets because they're sleepy. In a divorce, their egocentrism translates into the notion that somehow they are at the center of the problem. That they have "done" something and ought to be able to "undo" it. And that somewhere in this divorce lies the proof that they are bad, impotent or ineffectual.

Very young children, who are convinced of their central position in the universe, easily believe that had they only cleaned their room regularly, their parents would not be getting a divorce.

Slightly older children, who have a broader sense of cause and effect, still have trouble shaking off their feeling of responsibility. They may see a more meaningful indiscretion of theirs as contributing to the divorce, such as poor grades, high phone bills or mood swings, or may simply worry endlessly about what they might have done, unable to come up with anything satisfying.

But this egocentrism doesn't stop with figuring out the cause. It also invests children with a twisted sense of control over the outcome. A control they of course don't have but both enjoy and abhor contemplating. They enjoy it because it fills them with hope. They abhor it because it is a huge responsibility and one which they realize they cannot bear.

This is what sets the stage for why, apart from all the above fears and issues, children have such trouble asking what they need to know, and once they do, why it is so critical that parents learn what to say in response.

We cannot say this often enough: Children *must not* be abandoned to their own fantasies, because they will fear the worst about the situation and themselves. They cannot be left to fear abandonment or to see themselves as the cause of the divorce, for if they are, their entire sense of self will come into question. And they will not come out unscathed or undamaged.

They need help expressing themselves.

In a divorce, children of all ages have trouble asking the questions close to their hearts because they don't have the intellectual or emotional ability to formulate the issues and face their fears. And they don't have the confidence to believe they have a right to ask and an even greater right to know. The better able parents are to understand what holds their children back from seeking the information they so badly need, the easier it will be for them to answer the questions, both spoken and unspoken, in a way the children can tolerate.

Back to There's No Such Thing as a Simple Question

When it comes to divorce, then, it's easy to see why any question may not be quite what it appears. Certainly there will be truth to some queries: "Why does Daddy have to date?" may actually be a child's expression of confusion over his father's apparent desire to go out. But it may also mean, "Is that person going to be more important than me?"

This second question is a scary one. The child will worry the one true answer is yes. And so he is likely not to ask . . . that is if he's even aware of this deeper concern.

Unfortunately, though, he needs the answer to that secret question far more urgently than he does to the one that merely queries his father's romantic habits.

And that is the issue this book addresses.

Questions and answers. But not just the expressed questions and not just the specific answers. It also gets at the secret questions. The ones kids are too anxious or unaware to ask. And it suggests answers which every parent can use, with modifications for personality and circumstance, that both comfort and inform.

When a child is told he will always be loved by his father in a most special way but that as an adult his father needs other kinds of affection and warmth in his life, he is given the chance to consider that he is *not* replaceable. Other people cannot steal his love away. He is his father's son. Nothing can change that.

This reassurance will carry him a long way—through many a moment that might have left him wallowing in low self-esteem.

It is easy to see why the question-and-answer process is critical to children's ability to adapt to a divorce.

But before parents can begin, there is a job they must undertake in order to help their children as comfortably and constructively as possible. And that job is one they must do on themselves.

Divorce is a highly emotional process for everyone. But parents simply cannot afford to confuse their own feelings with those of their children.

Even if the children's fears are the same as theirs.

Even if the children are furious.

Even if the children blame them mercilessly.

Clear boundaries are essential.

And that is what the next chapter is about.

2.

Facing Your Own Questions First

Parents have questions about divorce too. Every day they bombard themselves with frightening, disheartening, angering and painful questions. Questions they cannot readily answer. (How am I going to manage financially?) Questions they can only bear to ponder for a few moments at a time. (Is it possible that no one will ever find me attractive again?) Questions that provoke such guilt or anger that a serious depression can set in for days. (Is this divorce the right thing? Could I have tried harder?) And questions that, like their children, they may be too scared or embarrassed to face at all. (Will I be alone forever?)

Divorce is a painful process. Researchers report it can take parents up to three years to adjust to all the changes a divorce can bring.

This adjustment would be hard enough for any adult coping with the loss of a central relationship, the upheaval of a lifestyle both financially and socially, and the struggle to redefine who he is and where he now fits.

But it becomes an even greater struggle when there are children involved. Questions of guilt arise. (Have I visited something upon my kids that will destroy them?) The time to reflect and self-heal is limited. (Why can't I find a few hours alone to just cry and think about the next step?) And the prospect of building a new life, with its limitations and caveats, can leave even the most devoted parent feeling guilty, if not horrified, over his secret thoughts. (I love my children so much, but is it normal that sometimes I wish they weren't my responsibility? That I could just take off? Cut loose? Start over?)

It's little wonder that parents may have trouble hearing, understanding and answering their children's questions. The cacophony of their own can be deafening.

The result? Parents may not intuit or listen with accuracy, leaving children neither free to express themselves nor sufficiently helped with their need to explore their fears.

It is very important that parents come to terms with their own questions and conflicts. Look at them. Know them. Predict them. And seek help for those they cannot cope with on their own. This is so certainly for their own sake. Parents, just like children, need to face their fears and anxieties. But it is so *most* importantly for the sake of their children.

Parents who know and understand themselves are far better able to help their children cope with their terrors than parents who are spending most of their energy repressing or dodging or being confused and victimized by their own fears. This becomes particularly true when a parent and child share a similar fear. How is a parent to help a child with a frightening thought if he or she is haunted by the same concern but unwilling to address it? The answer is, it can't be done.

Parents are not expected to have instant answers for calming themselves or soothing their children. But they do need to face all the possibilities, put them in perspective and offer hope, both to themselves and to their children. "I have no idea what you'll do this summer," is very different from, "I don't know whether you'll go to camp this summer, but we will definitely work out something for you that will be fun."

You are entitled, even as a parent, to be afraid, to question, to worry and to feel sad, angry or disappointed. These feelings needn't be a state secret. You can admit them to yourself and, in measured doses, to your child.

Your child will not suffer from the knowledge that you hurt. Your child will, however, suffer from your inability to face why you hurt and your subsequent inability to be open to his pain.

Phases of a Divorce and the Questions That Arise

As stated earlier, divorce is a process that takes place over several years. Just as the practical aspects of the divorce occur in phases (one spouse moves out, then perhaps a year later the house is sold, a new home is found, a new career is started), so do the emotions change with the phases.

If you are going to be open to what's troubling your children, if you are going to be intuitive about what they are picking up on or thinking, it's important to consider your own questions, as they reflect your changing fears, anger and hurt.

Starting with a kind of personal history will help shed some light on the issues that might deeply affect how you respond to your children's questions.

YOUR CHILDHOOD EXPERIENCES

Whether or not your parents ever separated or divorced, it is likely you have memories and attendant feelings about their marital relationship. It's a good idea to try and remember as much as possible about the observations, thoughts and fears that tripped across your mind as a child and adolescent. This has as much to do with understanding your child and your ability to listen and respond to him empathetically, as it does with understanding *yourself*. Following are some of the questions you should ask yourself:

• Did my parents fight a lot in front of me? How did I feel when they argued?

• Did I ever hear my parents say anything cruel to each other?

• Did I ever hear them screaming about me?

• Did I ever see my parents cry? What did I think then?

• When my parents separated did I give it a lot of thought or did I block it out?

• Did I talk to my parents about my feelings? If not, did I hold them in?

- Did my parents take my questions seriously or did they laugh or get annoyed?
- Did I think the world was falling apart when my parents divorced?
- Did I even understand what a divorce was?

You bring your past and present selves to every experience. The better you understand how the two are intertwined, the better able you will be not to repeat the mistakes of the past.

THE DOWNWARD SPIRAL

This is the period of time, while the marriage is still physically intact, during which there may be intense feelings of anger, tension, dissatisfaction, hurt and frustration. One or both parents are trying to decide if the time has come to separate. Filled with fears, reluctance, practical concerns and hurt, one or both partners may be wondering:

- How much longer can we go on like this?
- We try to hide the anger and tension, but can the children see?
- Will the tension and anger hurt the children?
- Can I face my friends if we separate?
- Does it mean I'm a failure or disloyal if I give up?
- Did we ever love each other?
- Am I to blame for what's happened?
- Did I drive him/her to leave?
- Why can't I control my rage?

• I don't want to hurt my husband/wife, but do I have to stay miserable?

• Will my children feel inferior, in some way, to the kids who come from intact families?

These and other questions haunt parents during the time when they are making the decision to part. It is a period of almost unbearable conflict, self-doubt and pain. Children are aware of the tremendous unrest in the house, but parents may be so consumed with their own indecision that they cannot address their children's feelings at all. And since it's a time when children are least likely to ask questions, since nothing concrete has happened, parents may wrongly assume they haven't noticed anything.

But many of the above questions have their counterpart in a child's head (Am I to blame for all their yelling? Why can't Mommy stop looking so sad?). If you are to help your children ask what they need to know, you need to place your questions alongside theirs. Again, you don't need all the answers. You just need to squarely face the issues from both your own and your children's perspectives so that you can offer comfort and well thought out explanations to your children.

THE BREAKUP OCCURS

This is the period during which one parent usually moves out. There is a concrete aspect, now, to what is happening to the family. Parents may experience everything from a short-lived elation to sheer panic. For both of them, there is a terrible emotional violence in this dramatic shift at home. One is left with the children, unsure of how to deal with the logistics of day-to-day matters. The other may find himself alone without the family that, despite the strife, has been the center of his life. Both parents are likely feeling ambivalent about what happens next. They may choose to go on autopilot in a vain attempt to push away the pain. At other times, utterly unsure of how to explain anything to the children, they struggle with their own questions:

- Are we ever going to get back together?
- Do I want to get back together?
- Do things have to change *that* much just because we've parted?
- I feel so frightened. What if I can't handle everything?
- Are we going to get back together out of loneliness instead of love?
- Should I tell the kids we're trying to work it out, even if I know we can't?
- I'm so angry. Do I want my kids to like their father/mother?
- How could I have done this to all of us?
- How am I going to manage single parenting?
- How am I going to feel not seeing my children regularly?
- Are the kids going to forget about me?
- Will my children hate me for leaving?
- Do I care if my kids have a good relationship with my soon to be ex?
- In my heart do I want them to hate him/her?
- Do I have a need to be the favorite?

The separation is traumatic to every family member. Whether a parent wants to leave or not, or even if he has another partner waiting, it's a shocking time. For children it's a clear, undeniable, physical sign that things have gone wrong. The questions begin coming slowly, largely off the point, but fearfully nonetheless. (Will Daddy be here for dinner tomorrow?) Parents need to address their own feelings of loneliness and abandonment and come to grips with some of their own often irrational feelings and fears, as they answer their children's questions. (Are you still going to be my Daddy? Why can't you try harder to work things out?) As difficult as the task might be, you will want to try and stay at least half a step ahead of your children. The more open you are to facing your own sense of abandonment and disorientation, the more capable you will be of helping your children with their similar feelings.

Children need to get the facts straight. It will help them feel more in control. But your answers do not always have to be answers per se. Often an acknowledgment of perceived reality is enough to satisfy children. They need information, but they also need to know that what they see is so. That way they can pour their energy into coping over time instead of hiding.

THE TRANSITION PHASE

Change is really settling in now—though "change" in this instance is a long process. The separation has become fact. A constant. But that's about the only thing that is. Life in many ways may be everything from slightly unstable to in a constant state of flux. Family members may be settled into new (if temporary) homes, but parents may be trying new partners, changing lifestyles in rapid succession (dating a lot, suddenly preferring to stay home, taking frequent weekend trips, staying home on weekends) and experimenting in other ways. This can be confusing for everyone. There is a sense, during this time, that things *should* be more settled. More predictable. More "normal." But, in fact, this lack of continuity is quite common. Parents may worry:

- Why aren't things coming together yet?
- Is any relationship I have going to work out?
- Can the children tell how off center I feel?
- Will I ever feel settled again?
- Have I kissed a "normal" family life good-bye with this divorce?
- How are my children going to feel running back and forth between two households?
- How am I ever going to get used to my kids sometimes not being home?
- Why am I relieved sometimes when my kids take off with their father/mother?
- Are my kids' problems at school due to the divorce or simply their stage of development?

This intense period of uncertainty, which is cloaked in a tentative new "routine," can leave parents worrying constantly, "What's wrong with me?" Children pick up the tension and translate it into fears of their own. "Something is wrong. What is it? Aren't I managing okay? Is it okay when I go off with Daddy? How come Mommy keeps switching boyfriends?" And, of course, secretly, "Will I be switched too?" Parents need to face their anxieties and work hard to adjust their expectations of both themselves and their children. The more realistic they are about the demands they make on themselves, the more available and aware they will be about the troubles their children face. If parents are able to arrive at a calm self-acceptance, it will help ease the children's demands upon themselves.

A NEW STABILITY

Time inevitably restores equilibrium to everyone's lives. Some parents have more permanent love relationships or find themselves remarried. Children are used to the new lifestyle as things have become far more predictable. New patterns are becoming set. They live in a single-parent home, live with stepfamilies or shuttle with predictable regularity back and forth between two different homes. It is during this phase that parents' questions may begin to subside and life becomes more regulated. With no small amount of relief they embrace their new lives and are now ready to put the sad times behind them. However, they must beware of this desire to put the divorce in the past, particularly for their children's sake. A parent who has found some measure of inner peace and who is grateful for its arrival may forget that the children are still dealing with the divorce in their own particular ways. They may be hurting, or actually dreaming that Mom and Dad will still get back together—even in the face of both parents having remarried.

Parents may not have that many questions left to haunt them during quiet times, but chances are there is still some nagging sadness, regret and anger that comes up from time to time. If they can recognize this in themselves, they will be better able to sense it in their children. They should think about the following:

• Have I explored any lingering guilt I have about what's happened to my family?
• Am I remaining open to my children's feelings, which might be different from my own?
• Are my children as happy or relieved as I think and hope they should be?
• Do I sometimes ignore my child's bad mood without trying to ascertain what it is about?
• Do I spend a lot of time pretending that everything is now all "fixed"?
• Do I have a right to feel this good?

It is critical for parents, navigating through this phase, to stay aware of how different the divorce experience is for their children and themselves. While relief may flood the parents, anguish may seize the children. While resolution might feel the hallmark of this period for the parents, deep sorrow might better describe the children's experience. Parents may feel inclined to put the bad times behind them in a way that almost denies they ever happened. This would be doing the entire family a dreadful disservice. The past stays with us in different ways and it must be acknowledged. Not held up before ourselves on a regular basis in the form of daily penance, but as a thread that will always be part of the tapestry of our lives. To leave out this thread would be to have a raveled and incomplete picture of our lives.

WHAT ABOUT THE GUILT?

There is a common feeling behind many of the questions parents have during the different phases of a divorce, and that is an overriding sense of guilt. What, they wonder, have they done to their children? To their spouse? To everyone's future?

Guilt is a very difficult emotion. If you don't admit it, it comes out in strange ways in odd places. Fits of anger over nothing, or terrible depression over nameless fears, are classic manifestations of guilt. On the other hand, the recognition of guilt is painful too. It can torture a person mercilessly. And once it gets started, it knows no boundaries. Guilt has a habit of spreading everywhere, in an insidious fashion.

Still, parents have to face it and deal with it. Almost no parents escape it. Nor should they. The cold reality is that they have made a difficult and painful decision primarily for themselves—a decision that usually causes great unhappiness and insecurity for their children, at least for a while. That *is* something to feel some amount of guilt over.

But the thing about guilt is that sometimes it's quite simply the downside of the right decision. Guilt is not necessarily an indication that "wrong" has been done. Rather, it is a reflection of an understanding that in taking action, pain has been caused. It can be the accompaniment of taking responsibility for a decision that leaves someone feeling terribly hurt. In fact, guilt is sometimes an incorrectly used word. "Sorrow" is more accurate. Also, perhaps, "misgivings." Sorrow for having been the power behind a difficult and painful decision. Misgivings for the natural concern and awareness of the pluses and minuses of any tough choice.

Such is life. Sometimes decisions have to be made which, while serving a good purpose, also cause pain. Guilt is part of the package—along with the knowledge that for the greater measure, the right move has been made. It is true there has been a betrayal. There exists, within the family, a kind of unwritten vow that it will be a permanent unit. And when a divorce strikes, it can feel like a stab in the back. This is hard for everyone to take. For the child a most basic "given" collapses. For parents, buried deep in their unconscious is a mandate to keep their children safe. When the decision to divorce is reached, the guilt can be overwhelming.

Parents need to face this guilt head on, and then to consider not only the facts that research has shown but also the facts in their particular homes.

So Have You Really Visited an Insurmountable Woe Upon Your Children?

That depends on the visit.

A divorce is an upsetting event. The way in which it is addressed within the family is critical.

The most common question on this subject is as follows: Isn't it better to simply stay together for the sake of the children no matter how bad the marriage?

The answer is no. Children are greatly harmed by a family unit rife with tension, anger, distrust, dissatisfaction and pain.

But the thing is they are also harmed by a divorce, rife with tension, anger, distrust, dissatisfaction and pain.

If the marriage is bad the children will feel it. If the divorce is *handled* badly (no divorce is "good") the children will feel it.

Children need understanding, nurturing, respect, parental cooperation, consistency, attention and love. They need it in an intact family and they need it when there is a divorce. If they don't get these things, serious far-reaching problems can take hold.

So, while the ideal situation is a marriage that works and a family that stays together with the glue of predictability, love and respect, if it doesn't work out it needn't signal the end of a child's well-being.

In fact—and this is not to comfort a parent unduly—many children, if a divorce is handled well, come out of the experience with personal strength, a healthy sense of the ups and downs of life and a faith in their own ability to triumph during hard times.

How Much of What You Feel Is Okay for Your Child to See?

Your child will not suffer irreparable damage by seeing your vulnerability. On the contrary, she may benefit from seeing you manage your fears and forge ahead. This is an important lesson. Life can feel terrible, but you needn't give up. You "feel" but you keep thinking, and you keep moving, and sooner or later the feelings and life will change. Like everything else, however, a child's reaction to your distress will depend on dosage and presentation.

Constant crying will, of course, upset your child as will a litany of "I just don't know what we're going to do" type statements. Your child will want to feel that you are in control of the situation and that she can count on you.

On the other hand, admitting to your child that you are worried too, and then enlisting her assistance with the problem, which you are sure has some resolution, will help her feel both connected to you and in control: "I feel sad too, but I think it will just take time for all of us to adjust to the change. Maybe we can think of something to do together to cheer us both up." Getting into the same boat with your child will comfort her tremendously.

If you are upset, you're bound to yell a little more, be somewhat preoccupied and inattentive, and at times completely lose your sense of humor. Your child will notice all of this, and how she handles it will have a lot to do with your honesty. Blowing your stack or ignoring your child and simply walking away will leave her feeling stranded. Explaining yourself won't. "I'm having a bad day, honey. Sorry I'm not listening so well," or "I woke up in a sour mood. I didn't mean to yell. It's not you," will go a long way towards comforting your child. She will feel both respected and included and you will be presenting yourself as a person who knows what's happening. You know yourself. You know your moods. Despite the moment, you're in control.

Finally, keep in mind it's the "victim" role that does everyone in. If you allow yourself to feel as if all of this has just "happened" to you and you'll have to wait for some good fortune to "happen" for the good times to roll, you're in trouble. It's the same for your child. It is far better to give her a sense that "doing" will help. Planning a trip, organizing a new afternoon schedule, beginning a Friday evening tradition of meatballs and spaghetti with ice cream sandwiches for dessert will translate into the idea that change is in your hands. And that change can be fun.

It Starts with You

Your child will take most of his cues from you.

If you remain a stranger to yourself, your child will probably not know how to make sense of what is going on around him. Let's face it. You are the guide. If the guide doesn't have a realistic sense of the terrain he is in, the travelers in his charge don't stand much of a chance.

Your child needs your help. And one of the first and most important steps you can take in providing that help is to face your own fears and concerns as you deal with your child's. It will give you more personal strength to face the problems ahead and will send the right messages to your child. He will sense your openness. The messages will be:

I'm with you. This is tough. But we'll get through.

I can handle your questions. Go ahead and ask.

I am in control. I may not be happy, but life is not falling apart.

I may not have the answers, but I don't mind thinking about it and trying to find some.

And, most importantly, you will be modeling a very important lesson to your child: He *can* and should face his fears. Running won't help.

All of you need to ask questions. The trick is how to encourage your children to express theirs.

That is the subject of the next chapter.

3.

How to Help Your Child Open Up

When it comes to communication, talking is not the tough part. The tough part is expressing what you really think or feel and helping someone else to do the same.

It's impossible, of course, to tell a person how to talk. People have their own rhythm, degree of openness, capacity to engage, comfort zone and facility with language. They also have their own moods and limits.

This is as true for adults as it is for children.

Still, there are some general principles a parent can follow to foster a constructive and caring conversation—no matter what the style of the individuals involved.

There are three stages in a warm, helpful and productive conversation.

You will want to:

• Create an atmosphere in which a conversation can take place.

• Listen in a way that encourages full expression, inspires trust and allows you to intuit that which remains hidden.

• Respond in a manner that shows empathy and offers comfort and help.

These three stages form the base of any fully productive conversation. Make them your goal. But keep in mind that anything short of a fully productive conversation could still be extremely useful.

Divorce Conversations Follow Their Own Drummer

Conversations about divorce are not likely to stay organized. There are too many emotions involved. Too many fears. You may experience yourself in a truly open conversation with your child, only to have him suddenly stand up and announce, midthought, he has homework. You may listen with a keen ear, reflecting your child's thoughts perfectly, only to hear him announce, "You don't understand anything!" Or you may have a deep, empathic understanding of your child's pain, but before you have a chance to get to some heartfelt encouragement you hear your child announce, "Actually, I'm not upset. I think this is just stupid. That's all."

Conversations about divorce take time and patience. Because of the nature of divorce, because it's a process, the discussions must also be a process. Feelings, thoughts, fears, conflicts and impressions will change from month to month. Sometimes even day to day. And the capacity to stick with a dialogue on such difficult subjects will change as well.

A Note About Timing, Silence and Too Much Too Fast

Timing is everything. You can't zoom in on your child just because you're in a reflective mood and expect she'll be right there with you. She may be worrying about something in school. She may be tired and hungry. It is critical to wait until the time seems right. Perhaps she wants to bring up something herself. Maybe the two of you are alone, feeling close, working on a puzzle together. Or, you might simply sense, while your child is chattering about something innocuous, that she is ready to take on a more weighty subject. The point is, you should try to maximize the probability that your child will engage in a conversation by catching her at a time when she is "available."

But always respect her silence. Certainly you can say things that are on your mind. If she doesn't get up and walk away, chances are she's listening. But if she says, "No, I don't want to talk about it," don't argue. You will increase the odds of her being ready to talk if she understands it's her call. Pushing a child to express herself will not get at her feelings. It will only bring out her defensiveness and anger. As a result, she will be unlikely to listen to a word you say, no matter how helpful.

Be aware, also, of the power of suggestion. There may be times when you're tempted to ask a question for your child. She's been too quiet. She needs help getting started. You may be right.

It is, however, a tricky line that must be walked. A poorly asked question on behalf of a child can precipitate her fears. Asking a five-year-old if she's afraid she'll never see Daddy again may be equal, in her mind, to telling her that in fact this might happen. "I wonder if you're worrying about how much you'll see Daddy?" will be far more useful and elicit a much more informative response from your child.

The Three Stages

Review the following steps carefully, but understand they do not add up to a definitive conversation about divorce. That is just about impossible. The best of dialogues may need to take place over and over, with little changes here and there, before the full message comes through. Nor are the suggested "scripts" supposed to represent the ideal words. There are none. The sample dialogues are here to illuminate the way particular words or phrases can, while on the surface seeming innocuous, communicate something more significant or unintended. And they are also here to offer suggestions that parents might use, in their own fashion, to illustrate their acceptance of and openness to their children.

The ultimate goal of the steps that follow is to get your child to talk, to help him feel cared for and respected, and to find a way to communicate your support and your willingness and ability to help him through the divorce experience.

STEP ONE: FACILITATING A CONVERSATION

We've established that children yearn deeply for the answers to their questions. Unfortunately, many things get in the way. Fear, conflict, guilt, limited language skills, etc. But there is another thing too.

It's hard to start a conversation. Especially one that's filled with potential angst. You may have a child who says she wants to talk but then gets stuck discussing things that matter little to her. Or, you may have a child who simply looks at you, as if in great pain, but is unable to get a word out. Then, too, you may have a child who walks about as if she is oblivious to what's happening, except that you notice she's avoiding you quite a bit. Finally, you could have a child who presents you with all three of these "personae," depending on the week.

Since each style creates its own challenge, we've given different advice for each.

THE CHILD WHO BRINGS UP EVERYTHING BUT THE KITCHEN SINK . . . AND THE DIVORCE

Your child may know deep down that there's something she needs to talk about, but she doesn't quite know what it is. Or, she may know but is too afraid to bring it up. So she approaches you about one thing or another. It is likely she will linger near you even after the conversation is over, clearly wanting something else but too afraid to ask. So help her. But not too fast, and not too aggressively. There's a reason she's not getting it out herself. She's not sure . . . about anything.

• Study her with interest. Don't allow yourself to be

distracted, no matter how boring or off the point the conversation seems to you.

• Make it clear you would welcome any conversation with her on any subject. Ask her, "So, is there something else on your mind?" or "Well, I'm glad we covered that. What else?"

• If your child looks distressed, gently say, "You know, you look like something else more serious is on your mind. I'd be happy to talk about whatever it is, honey. Really."

• Draw on the obvious, so that it's clear the problems at home do not have to be an "untouchable" between you. When there is a pause at the conclusion of a conversation, you might try, "I'm glad we're talking, because I've been meaning to say to you that I know things have been a little tense around here. I imagine you've felt that?" Then, whether you get a nod or not, you could add, "Would you like to know what's happening?"

THE CHILD WHO LOOKS STRICKEN, OR BEHAVES ANGRILY, BUT WON'T TALK

The silence is probably caused by tremendous fear and anger. But it in no way reflects a lack of yearning for answers. Your child needs them desperately (though he may not be aware of it) and will have to be drawn out carefully and with great patience.

• Use non-accusatory observations or *reflective* statements as a springboard. These are remarks that address the situation but don't impose a judgment of any kind. "I'm not sure, honey, but you look a little sad to me. Is something on your mind?" Or, "You know, I feel like that look on your face is an angry one. Do you want to tell me what's bothering you?" Saying, "You look angry," or "Why do you look so sad?" can come across as a frontal attack. It is more effective to couch your observations with an admission that this is only how you see things.

• Again, don't shrink from the obvious. Introduce it but try to keep the drama factor low. Don't say, "You look miserable! You must be upset about something!" These words are too frightening in their intensity. Instead, say, "Honey, I can tell something is on your mind. It seems to me there's been a lot of yelling around here. Do you want to talk about that? I would if I were you." Or, "You look a little sad to me. I wonder if it has to do with Daddy. Are you missing him a little?" If you bring out options your child might feel less scared to express his own thoughts.

• Help him see his anger for what it is. "You know, you're getting very angry about stuff that I have a feeling is not so important to you. Do you think maybe you're really upset about something else?"

• Bring yourself into the story as a symbolic companion. Draw on your own experience for common ground. "Sometimes when I'm very unhappy about something I yell a lot about smaller things because I'm just in such a bad mood about big things. Is it like that for you?" By creating a camaraderie between the two of you, you will help your child feel more connected, less alone and more trusting.

• If a child is consistently silent, it will be hard to figure out the exact moment for you to draw him in. Let him know on a regular (but not nagging) basis that you are open to talking whenever he is. "I have a feeling some things are on your mind. There's a lot going on at home. If you want to talk about anything just tell me." Or, "I know you must be wondering about what's going to happen now. You're not talking much, but I'm sure it's on your mind. It's certainly on mine. I'd be happy to talk to you about things. Whatever you've got on your mind is fine." The point is to let your child know that when he's ready, you will be too.

THE CHILD WHO ACTS AS IF LIFE IS THE SAME AS IT'S ALWAYS BEEN

This is an extremely well-defended child—at least for the moment. Which means he won't act scared, he won't act sad and he won't act angry. He'll just walk around avoiding everything. He is, however, bound to start leaking pain somewhere sometime. You will want to help him do it in as focused a way as possible.

Be prepared, however, for the brick wall you are likely to come up against as you inch forward!

• Appreciate that first you have to get him to acknowledge there are even things to talk about! That in itself might be a huge task. Silence, for a child, is a way of staying in control.

• Recognize he's not going to be ready to talk just because you feel ready to draw him out. In fact, he may be a long way away from talking at all. You might have to settle at first for a series of truncated conversations that only lightly touch on the important issues.

• Don't buy his denials, but don't dismiss them either.

If you begin with, "Honey, I was wondering if you've no-ticed anything funny between Daddy and Mommy lately," or "Sweetie, you haven't said much about how different it feels now that Daddy isn't here," don't give up if your child says, "No, I haven't," or "It feels fine." You'll just be playing his game. And don't say, "That's not true," or "I know you feel bad." It's too intrusive and very presumptuous. Even if you're right, it is unrealistic to expect a child who is pouring all his energy into hid-ing to suddenly turn around and cry out, "Yes! That's true!" Instead, nod and try saying something like, "Well, I know that Daddy and I haven't been getting along that well and I'm pretty sure you've heard us yelling. I won-der if you want to ask me about that." Or, "I think it feels strange without Daddy around. . . ." The point is, your child has to acknowledge the problem before he can bring himself to talk about it.

• Try using play items and activities such as clay, board games, drawing or puppets to get your child talk-ing. You don't need to be a skilled child psychologist to sit and draw a group of people with your child and to comment, "The little boy sure looks angry over there in the corner." Such activities can serve as a very effective springboard to conversation.

• Don't insist in the face of a brick wall. If you are get-ting nowhere and your child consistently denies every-thing, growing increasingly more upset as you press, step away. Drop it. He's not ready. But as you walk away, warmly and matter-of-factly say something like, "Okay. Well, if something does start to bother you, please come and talk to me about it. I love you and I want to help you with things that trouble you."

Starting up a conversation about a difficult matter is no easy task. Especially when there's temptation from both parties to play dodgeball. It is also, in many ways, the trickiest part of a potentially helpful conversation. Creating the opportunity for your child to open up is highly dependent on the sort of child you have and his particular frame of mind. Keep in mind you're not a mind reader. Your attempts at conversation may fall totally flat, but that needn't herald doom. Just keep trying!

The following techniques, for steps two and three, can be used with most children. Listening and responding constructively are skills which even the most "available" parent needs to hone on a consistent basis. There is a fine line between the two, but for purposes of clarity we're going to separate them here.

STEP TWO: LISTENING TO WORDS AND MORE

You can't fake listening. You know when a friend is giving you her full attention and when her mind is elsewhere. You know it intuitively from the look in her eye, her body language and the words she chooses to acknowledge what you are saying. Children pick up these things as well.

The most important thing that you need to project to your child when she is talking is *acceptance*. This is different from approval or agreement. Those things are important and, if honestly felt, make a child feel good. But *acceptance* of how she feels and what she thinks is most critical, because it allows her to be who she is, independent of what you are or think. She knows she doesn't have to say or do what you want, for her to be appreciated. Following are some things you can do to show your child that you accept her for who she is and what she feels.

• Use your body, not just your eyes, when talking with your child. Put down the newspaper when she approaches you. Turn away from the television when you sense your child is trying to tell you something other than the fact that she's finished her homework. Give your child the kind of full attention she can see as well as feel.

• Let her finish. Don't interrupt. Don't jump into the middle of her thoughts with your own interpretations. "Yes. I know what you mean. It's like . . ." just won't do. The act of getting the words out is just as important as knowing what they are and that one wants to say them. Your child deserves and needs the release of expressing her own thoughts, her way, in her own time.

• Encourage her to feel that you're listening and to continue, by nodding and saying such things as, "I see," "Mmm, hmmm" or "Go on." She will interpret these comments as proof that you are indeed paying attention.

• Acknowledge your child's right to her feelings, no matter how it makes you feel or what you think she should think. Comments such as "That's silly," or "You couldn't have felt like that," or "You should never feel that way," are forms of denial. They are a way of telling your child that what she feels is "wrong." The goal should be for her to know she is entitled to her feelings, whatever they might be.

• Offer reflective statements. These are observations that indicate you are listening and "getting it." "I can see you feel very frustrated," or "You are feeling very angry," are examples. Be careful, however, not to overstate an emotion. "You are absolutely furious!" or "You feel so horrible!" while seemingly warm and emotional, are theatrical statements. You don't want to respond to the potential drama of a situation. You want to respond to the core feeling.

STEP THREE: RESPONDING WITH EMPATHY AND HELP

As stated earlier, all children need to feel accepted. But along with this, they need something else. They need to feel understood. They need it for validation, and they need it to serve as a sort of engine. If children feel understood, they will be more likely to summon up the courage to keep talking.

Empathic or compassionate responses flow when parents allow themselves to feel for their children and to express this very sensitive understanding in a way that allows the children to feel "known."

• Let your child see you have a sense of what his life feels like. If your child tells you sadly, just after being dropped off by his father after a weekend visit, "I want to be by myself for a little while," you might try nodding and saying, "You look a little sad. Saying good-bye is hard, even if it's just for a short while."

• Respond with feeling. Words such as, "I can see you're angry," or "Don't you look unhappy," don't work if they are said matter-of-factly or unaccompanied by a sympathetic look or gesture. Your child will feel dismissed, and rightly so. Empathy is not simply an intellectual understanding of a feeling; it's also an emotional one that requires the listener to express warmth.

• Stay with the feeling along with your child. Sometimes parents, in their natural desire to shield their children from unhappiness, try to rush them away from a difficult feeling. It isn't fair to say, "I can see you feel sad, and I'm sorry, but just think, tomorrow we're going to the beach." If your child is brave enough to stay with a bad feeling, so should you be. This will convey a critical lesson about life. Sadness happens. You have to allow for it. It will go away only when you give it a chance to breathe. The idea is to give thoughts and feelings full flower, so that fantasies and fears can be clarified and understood. This is a process that takes time. If you rush, you'll miss the opportunity.

• Don't press for explanations. It will create tension in a child who may not know exactly what is bothering him. If your child walks in distressed and says something to indicate the fact, don't immediately ask, "Why do you feel this way?" Rather, use an observation or reflective statement. "You look so unhappy," said with great feeling, will help him feel accepted and set the stage for him to reflect on his own reasons.

Offering Help

When children come to their parents with a problem, they should find acceptance, understanding and help. This "help" is not simply providing a solution. It should also assist the children as they develop their own ability to help themselves. Obviously, if a child comes to a parent over a fight with a friend, or fearful of a piano recital, the discussions and solutions will be finite and somewhat concrete in nature. When it comes to divorce, because it is a process and because things are often uncertain and unknown, concrete assurances or resolutions are not always possible.

The most realistic goal in terms of "help" is the promise of hope and the sense that time will ease many of the changes that now seem so awkward, painful and sudden. Of course, offering some immediate short-term answers will also help.

• Give your child a chance to find solutions. "I can see it hurts you when Daddy arrives late to pick you up. Maybe we could tell him in a way that's comfortable for you." Let your child consider this for a moment, and if nothing is suggested you can step in.

• Always suggest more than one possibility. You might try "Maybe a note? Or, maybe when you talk to him next on the phone you could ask him to come right on time. You could say, 'Daddy, please come at six like you said. It's hard waiting for you.' " Choices will help your child keep control and focus on what really feels best to her.

• If nothing can be done about a particular problem, acknowledge the pain, let her know you can see why she feels the way she does, and then assure her things will get better. "I know this room is much smaller than your old one. I guess that makes you miss the way things used to be." Then add something like, "But you know it's a funny thing about a person's own room. No matter how big or small, once you get used to it, it becomes a very private, special place. I have a feeling that will happen with this new room. But you each have to get to know each other first."

• Be careful not to reply with your own needs in mind. You may want your child to cheer up, but she may need to be down. You may wish for her to socialize with all her friends, but she may need to be alone. When talking to your child, resist suggestions that would give you a lift. If she tells you she'd rather be alone than hang out with the kids, don't say, "But honey! You usually have such a good time with them." Maybe she doesn't want to have a good time right now. Clearly, if this becomes a habit you will want to seek help for her, but if your child is in a "mood," don't try to fix it. The mood itself may be serving an important purpose for her. She might be giving herself room to feel bad. In the end, that's the only way she'll feel better.

Families of Non-talkers

Some families have a history of non-communication.

They don't talk. Or sometimes they do, but about more shallow matters. Opening up discussions about heavy emotional topics does not come easily. There is often too much repression or inhibition in the family, and perhaps too little psychological know-how to address the problem.

The emotional upheaval of a divorce will not turn this around, but it will put a great deal of pressure on the family to change its basic dynamic. Children, no matter how they have learned to be in the family, will need to have their fears and fantasies addressed. And parents will have to help them.

Families that are unaccustomed to exploring their feelings together might find it necessary to seek professional help. It is also likely that the parents in this sort of family will need to seek individual help in facing their own problems as they move on to help their children. Again, parents who remain unaware of or unresolved about their problems will not easily see their children's needs.

No One Says the Right Thing All the Time

You cannot legislate how one person will respond to another. Too much depends on mood, style, timing, ability to express oneself, personality and more.

Also, everyone has their weaknesses and strengths. Knowing the most constructive response does not always mean you will be able to give it. Tension, fatigue or just plain impatience may render parents incapable of coming up with the best words during a stressful, or even quiet, moment. Children, too, will be subject to their own foibles. A particularly high-strung child may be extremely unpredictable. One day she may react positively to your smoothly orchestrated opening, and on another she may turn on you with surprising venom.

Conversations may be peppered with your own "mistakes": accusations (You're so selfish), defensiveness (I am not. Don't ever say that again!), resentment (You don't care how I feel), too much inquiry (How could you possibly say that to me?), too little understanding (I think that's ridiculous) and more. It's all part of being a human being immersed in a very difficult situation.

The goal is to concentrate as much as possible on being available and accepting. The overall attitude will always win out over the glitches that might occur on any given day. Mistrust does not come from a minor skirmish. It comes from a prolonged period of inattention and denial. Besides, you can always go back and correct a misstep: "Remember the other day when I said you shouldn't say those things? That was wrong of me. You have a right to say how you feel. I was very tired. It had nothing to do with you."

Above all else, your conversations about divorce should be honest and realistic.

That will inevitably entail some imperfections.

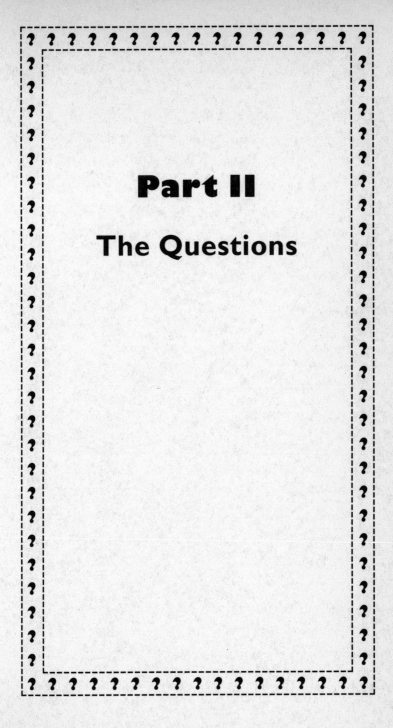

Part II

The Questions

4.

How to Use What Follows

Part 2 of this book covers the many questions kids ask during the divorce process. Keeping in mind both clinical and personal experience, and editorial constraints, certain decisions had to be made in order to lay out the material in a useful and organized manner.

Life, clearly, doesn't come so neatly packaged.

When reading part 2, you will need to keep in mind the following points.

•These "Question" chapters follow the phases of a divorce. We have tried to place each question during the phase when it is most likely to surface, but since divorce talks are so unpredictable, it's best to review all the chapters in case your child zooms in on an issue that for the most part "comes later."

•There are many questions that presuppose the mother is the parent being addressed. This is because most children live with their mothers after a divorce and are thus more apt to have serious conversations with her than their father. It is also true that they have probably had greater experience talking with her about emotional topics. Whenever appropriate, realistic or particular to the father-child relationship, we have directed the question towards the father. For the most part, however, either parent can answer the question.

•The questions and answers come from and go to boys or girls in largely arbitrary fashion. Certainly there are some issues that boys are more comfortable discussing with their fathers and girls with their mothers, but the answers, philosophically and psychologically, are interchangeable and can be given by either sex parent. A boy who asks his father if he's sleeping with a woman ought to receive the same answer as a girl who queries her mother about her sex life. A mother who needs to help her son keep his oedipal impulses under control would follow the same road as a father confronted by a daughter who wants to spend the entire evening in his lap.

•As mentioned in part 1 of this book, all sample "scripts" are offered mainly for approach. Each parent needs to put things into their own words. Certainly it's important to incorporate the most helpful comments, encouragements and suggestions, and even more important to be aware of the minefields, as pointed out in each question. But you need to adapt your language and answers to your own style, your child's age and temperament, and the particulars of the situation.

•While the scripts needn't be repeated word for word, you do need to focus on the suggested ways to answer a question that has not exactly been asked and that may not even be in the conscious mind of the child—though he desperately needs the answer. It might be easier to conclude, "He's not worried about that!" But what if he is? It can't hurt to assure him of something he already knows. But it can hurt to ignore something he doesn't.

•While we obviously have not been able to include each specific question that every child might ask, many of the answers contain general points that may be used in other related questions. For instance, a child who asks, "Why do you want to get married again?" might need an answer similar to that for, "Why do you have to date?" Or, a child who says, "Is it okay if I like Daddy's girlfriend?" needs to hear much of what you would say if he asked, "Why are you so bad-tempered when I come back from visiting Daddy and Michelle? Isn't that okay?"

Read all the questions and answers. Somewhere, you will find an approach to the question that your child has suddenly thrown your way.

•The tone of all the answers on these pages is even, tolerant and loving. It isn't always possible to be tolerant and loving in real life. Sometimes you will be feeling too vulnerable and upset yourself to offer answers with equanimity and self-assurance. That's okay. Just try to keep "to the program" as much as possible. A little more or less tension or obvious upset as you respond to a question won't hurt. In fact, it will remind your child that you're a person too and that you're in this together. But if you do let things get out of hand and respond with excessive, unhelpful emotion, acknowledge it to your child later: "I shouldn't have said those things. What I said about Daddy isn't really true. I was feeling terrible and I just let all sorts of thoughts fly." Knowing you are back in control will help your child place the moment in perspective.

• Finally, recognize that a divorce affects children in many different ways. Some can tolerate the inherent pain and confusion better than others. The same is true of adults. If you do not seem readily able to communicate or be open and honest with each other, and if your child seems consistently down, it would be wise to consult a professional. The questions and answers in this book will go a long way towards helping parent and child understand each other during the divorce process. But the material here can't resolve deep-seated pain, insecurity or unhappiness that probably predated the actual separation. A professional, however, can help to get at those issues that are making the divorce experience so intolerable.

5.

The Dark Days Before the Break

A seriously troubled marriage will usually create an equally troubled atmosphere in the home. Even if you manage to keep obvious anger or frustration under control, people of all ages will feel the problem. Your children will "know," consciously or otherwise.

The question is, what will they know?

A lot of that will depend on what they witness. But a lot of it won't. A lot of it will spring from where they are in age, emotionally and developmentally, and their own individual personalities. How much they notice, what they notice, and what they make of what they notice will be molded by the idiosyncratic nature of who they are and what's actually taking place in their lives.

The most important point is that you should not allow yourself to become lulled into "a false sense of privacy." You are a family. And family members know things even if few or no words are spoken.

• Yelling angrily behind closed doors when the children are asleep, in order to avoid detection, is but an illusion. The children may not be asleep, or they may simply wake up as your voices reach a fevered pitch. A closed door muffles sounds but not emotions.

• Allowing an angry confrontation to take place in front of the children, and then simply offering an "It's nothing. Daddy and I are fine" will increase, not decrease, your child's anxiety. Denials in the face of the facts don't protect children. Rather, they terrify them. What, they think, could be so bad that Mommy and Daddy have to try and trick me?

• A steady tension in the house, with no angry words but no exchange of warmth and affection between husband and wife, is a palpable thing. Children may not be able to put into words what they sense is wrong, but they will experience the oppression and it will drag them down if the facts are not brought forth.

• "Whispered conversations" on the phone with friends or family about the troubles in your marriage might just as well, after a while, be on a P.A. system. Children move in and out of rooms. They even intentionally and successfully eavesdrop, especially when they sense they shouldn't.

There are no real secrets in a family. But there is a lot of pretending.

And that's just what you want to avoid.

This difficult phase, when a decision about separating or divorcing has not been reached, or has been but neither party is quite ready to "act," is a unique time in the divorce process for children.

Unlike in the phases that follow, there are few concrete indications at this time that the marriage is over. Children have the time to spin any fantasy, dream any dream, fear any fear and wish any wish. In some ways this is good. If the marriage is not over, there is always room for hope and children should be allowed their fair share.

Unfortunately, parents are tempted during this time to try to hide the problems. This only makes the children stay silent, not rock the boat and hope that everything will be just fine.

This doesn't work for anyone.

Whether there is hope or not, if the family is still intact despite a terrific undercurrent of unrest, life at home could be everything from uncomfortable to relentlessly painful. Questions are bound to build, along with the desperate hope that all of this trouble will just go away.

As a result, this is one phase of a divorce during which children are unlikely to chance too many questions. Not even ones that vaguely skirt the issue. From their perspective, unless there is an immense amount of emotional or physical violence, it is far better to try to repress what they fear and wish for what they most want.

Parents, emotionally exhausted from indecision and tension, may be unable and unwilling to even consider how their children feel. In fact, their children's silence may feel like a welcome gift.

But the truth is, this is an important time for openly introducing the reality of a problem.

If the marriage turns out to be fixable, you will have taught your children a lesson about recognizing pain,

dealing with it openly and finding resolutions. If it ultimately is not reparable, you will have used this time
wisely by setting the stage for what was to come. (There
are some instances, which we will get to later, in which
a parent suddenly announces he is leaving. In such
cases, shock is unavoidable. This will be covered in the
next chapter.)

This first, critical, phase is tricky to navigate because
parents must talk about matters that are not concrete.
Concrete matters are not easier to speak about, but at
least they usually assume that both parties are looking at
the same set of facts. During this phase, when no one
has moved, parents will need to draw their kids out on
the subject of what "might" be happening and how people are feeling. Children may resist or strongly deny.
(The one exception to this is the problem in which parents have decided to divorce but are still under the same
roof, sleeping in separate rooms.)

You will note, in this phase, unlike in the rest, parents
share the "task" of asking the questions with their children so that everyone can begin to face what is going on
at home. It is a transition period from illusion to reality
and your children will need you to serve as guide.

The Time to Talk

Whether you're still somewhat hopeful despite the tension, or quite convinced someone will soon be moving
out, it is critical to find some way to introduce the subject that does not frighten your child, but which offers
him some understanding of what is going on in the
household.

●

*You and your husband have been fighting regularly be-
hind closed doors. You have been fairly sure your children are oblivious. But now it's the morning after a
particularly vituperative argument and your four- and
eight-year-old sons seem listless at the breakfast table.*

If you choose to talk with them together, sit down
calmly at the table. Look each of them in the eye in a
manner that says you are not afraid to face their
thoughts or feelings. And then do the opposite of what
you might be tempted to try. Don't ask, "Did you hear
anything last night?" That is a test. That will put your
children on the spot. They're not sure they're "allowed"
to hear what they did. And they are also hoping it was
all a bad dream. By asking them this question you are
giving yourself and them an out.

Rather, in a soft voice, try something like, "Daddy and
I have been arguing quite a bit lately, haven't we?" This
statement will feel far less threatening to your children.
You are inviting them to agree with you about something
that they surely feel but might be afraid to bring up.

You may get any one of several reactions.

Your older child, in particular, might deny hearing a
thing, and the younger might simply mimic him. "No, I
didn't hear anything," each might claim. And then they
might make a slip. "We were sleeping."

Nod, and keep pushing forward gently. "Well, sometimes even when a person is sleeping they can hear a lot
of real-life noisy stuff going on in the other room. And
sometimes it can wake them up." You might then add,

"But I'm not just talking about last night. I'm talking about the fact that Daddy and I have been arguing a lot even in the day."

If the children insist they know or have heard nothing, don't play their game. But don't force them to play yours either. They may need time alone to think about what you've said. Just offer a few facts, making it clear you don't need a response. "Well, there has been some arguing and I think you guys have probably heard it. I just want to say that Daddy and I are definitely having a few problems getting along right now, but we both do want to try and work out our differences. It isn't easy, though. And it must be hard to hear. If you have any questions about it at any time just let me know, and I'll try to answer them."

By doing this, you will have introduced into the open that you and their father are having problems, that you want to fix them and that you don't feel good about this and understand it must be hard to watch. You will have given your children permission to know more, and to feel bad, but to retain their hope.

If your younger child, who might be less well defended, decides to be honest by saying, "Yes. I hear you fight. Why do you fight so much?" be as straight as you can. And recognize that your older child is listening to your answer with every fiber of his being. "We're fighting because we disagree about lots of things," you might offer.

"Like what?" he might say.

This is a tricky question. Younger children, especially, would find it nearly impossible to understand many of the reasons adults argue. You yourself may not be clear on all the reasons. And during this phase, when you and your husband might be struggling to work things out, you might feel especially reluctant to even imply a particular cause. "We argue about how to do things," you might try. "You know, like you and your friends sometimes fight about how to play a game, or what you both want to do for the afternoon? Well, parents sometimes do that too." In this way, you will not have made your business his, but you will have related it to something he can understand. That's what your child really wants. He's not as concerned with the details of your fight as he is with the feeling that it is something unknown or scary.

During this conversation—or non-conversation, depending on how open your children are at the moment—you will want to add something like, "I want you to know our fights are not about you. They're not your fault. You two are great and we love you both very much." Again, children of all ages can be very egocentric. They need to be told, over and over, that they are not the cause of your problems.

◑

You and your wife have been arguing intensely in the house. Each time the two of you go at it, your thirteen-year-old runs into his room and slams the door.

Wait for a quiet time with your adolescent or teen. Don't try to grab him directly after a fight, when he might be feeling extremely raw. Don't squeeze it in between his activities so that he has a perfect excuse to cry, "Gotta go! I'm late!" And don't do it just when you're in the mood to face his defenses. Rather, wait to catch your child in a moment of calm. He might be in his room, reading, or sharing a light dinner with just you or your wife as well.

"Look," you might begin. "I know Mom and I have been fighting a lot. I'm sorry you have to hear it. It must be very upsetting."

If your adolescent says, "I don't care," with a major-league shrug, respect his defense but make it clear you aren't fooled.

"I have a feeling that's not entirely true," you might say. "It's not pleasant hearing your parents talk to each other the way we do. If you don't want to talk about this right now it's okay, but I'd be happy to another time. Mom and I are definitely having our problems and there isn't any reason for us to pretend we're not. This happens sometimes in a marriage."

You will also want to offer a quick statement about what you're doing to correct things. "Mom and I are working on it and we hope to get through this rough period soon. We don't like the situation either."

By talking frankly and openly to your child you may not inspire him to ask a lot of questions and express his fears, but you will begin to take the "unspeakable" edge off the situation. Your willingness to talk and acceptance of the problem as a part of your life will help him begin to accept it as a part of his. A part he doesn't have to shrink from. And a part he can be sad but hopeful about.

The Dark Days Before the Break

There has been a lot of strife in your house and your son tearfully cries out, "Why don't you guys stop it already!"
Hidden questions:

- *Why can't you get in control?*
- *Why do you have to keep scaring me like this?*
- *Do you think I'm invisible?*

This is a moment that would give any parent great pause. It's a genuine expression of a need for peace, attention and security. Your child senses them slipping away and he wants them back.

The trouble is, you can't give them to him right now. Or at least not in a way that he remembers ever existing in his life before. This is bound to be a painful fact for both of you.

You can, however, apologize and promise that you will try to get your behavior under control. An apology that centers on the way you have acted is a way of telling your child he has a right not to be frightened or upset by painful expressions of your problems. You respect and agree with his desire to defend himself and to expect some degree of protection from his parents' problems.

"I'm sorry. Daddy and I have been fighting too much and certainly too much in front of you. It's not fair. We need to work out our problems in a way that isn't so hurtful to everyone. And we will try to do that."

You will also want to be clear that your child means a great deal to you even though you have apparently been ignoring his presence. "Daddy and I have been so angry we've sometimes forgotten what it must feel like for you to hear our fights. We love you very much, but I think we get caught up in our anger sometimes and we forget to pay attention to your feelings. You have a right not to be upset by us, especially because it has nothing to do with you."

If you are seeing a therapist or some other guidance professional, there is nothing wrong with telling this to a child of any age. For the younger ones, you might try, "Daddy and Mommy are going to see a helping person. This is someone who helps us talk about our problems and maybe find ways to get along better. You know how sometimes when you have a fight with a friend, it helps if another person talks to both of you to help calm things down? Well, that's what this helping person is trying to do for Daddy and me."

If the child is older, you can simply say, "We want you to know we're seeing a marriage counselor because we want to try and work out these problems. It's tough going, which is why we're still fighting. But we'll talk about that at our next appointment and try to improve things."

Then add, "We're glad you complained. You shouldn't have to take all of this in silence." And to the younger child you might add, "Thanks for telling us to stop shouting. I like to know how you feel."

Your children need to know, directly, that you are glad to hear them express even their most angry, critical or unflattering thoughts and feelings.

◗

You and your wife are experiencing so much tension that you have occasionally begun sleeping in different rooms. Your older daughter has said nothing about this, but your younger suddenly pipes up on the way to school with, "How come you sometimes sleep in the den now, Daddy?"

Hidden questions:

- *Does it mean something important?*
- *Should I be bothered by this?*

For the younger child, the marital bed is simply the expected place where Mommy and Daddy go at night. If the pattern is broken she may sense there's something "wrong," but not necessarily feel too threatened. This is why she is able to ask the question.

The answer you provide should be equal to her basic, available concept of husband and wife. "Well, you know how sometimes when you have a good friend but you get into an argument you sort of have to walk away? Spend some time without that person? Well, when Mommy and I fight we sometimes need to be away from each other too, for a little while. We're trying to make it so we don't feel so angry, though."

Your younger child will usually accept this explanation, though your sleeping separately will still not sit comfortably with her. She may bring it up with you again, or even announce to her friends, "My Mommy and Daddy don't always sleep in the same room. Isn't that funny!" These reactions will simply be her way of trying to make room in her life for what she hopes is a temporary change. And a tacit way of admitting she realizes it may not be so funny at all.

Your older child recognizes, however, that the marriage bed is a potent symbol. If the two of you aren't in it together, it means serious trouble. But because it is such a sensitive subject, she will probably elect not to ask any questions. She will simply watch, filled with anxiety, as this uncomfortable new ritual takes hold. Again, you will want to wait for a calm time when the two of you are alone and she is more likely to be available to you.

"I guess you noticed I have been sleeping in the den sometimes?" you might try.

She is likely to say, "Not really," or "I guess," or "It doesn't matter."

Just keep moving forward but with a sensitivity to her potential embarrassment. She knows that if you're sleeping in separate beds you are not having sex, and while no teenager is comfortable with the thought of her parents' sexuality, she is comforted by the fact that at least they are experiencing it in each other. That they are loving to each other.

"Well, I just want you to know that it's happening right now because we're having trouble getting along. We're trying to work our problems out, but right now we need to get a little extra space from each other. Hopefully we'll both feel better about each other soon, but I can't be sure when that will be."

Keep in mind that no matter what the age of the child, all children feel warm and secure when there is obvious physical affection between parents. While they may roll their eyes, or yell out "Stop it!" when the two of you kiss, it is still a sign to them that all is well in their home. Their fueling station. Their safety net.

When signs of physical affection begin to disappear, children of any age notice. They worry and wonder and may even grow more affectionate with you to fill up the "space." It's not a bad adaptive response as long as they do not overdo it. If your son tries to crawl into bed with you regularly, or snuggles up to you constantly throughout the day, you will want to make it clear that you don't need that sort of attention from him. "You're my sweet son. I love getting kisses from you, but it's time for you to go off and read your book," or "This is Daddy and Mommy's bed, honey. You go off to yours."

It should be noted, too, that a parent's need for extra affection during this time may be intense. Unintentional mixed messages might be sent to the child. Messages that say, "I feel lonely. You can't fix that. But still, I'd love a hug." It is a complex loneliness which a parent might be experiencing at this time, and not one a child can help to alter. Try not to "ask but not ask." Your child will become confused and could end up suffering from feelings of inadequacy.

◗

You and your husband are having a rather intense argument and he suddenly storms out the door. Your seven- and twelve-year-old sons are well aware he's gone but spend the evening watching TV and doing their homework. Finally, after you've tucked your seven-year-old into bed, he begins to cry. You walk into his room. "Where's Daddy?" he whimpers.

Hidden questions:

- *Is he coming back?*
- *Is he safe?*
- *Why would he leave me? What did I do?*

Any time parents walk out of the house without letting children know where they are going or why, it can feel like a desertion. There is an unspoken contract between parent and child, a kind of invisible string that keeps them bound together. If they cannot see each other but know where the other is, the distance is acceptable. Each can be called back. Each can be seen again.

But when a parent simply walks out without an explanation, it can feel, to a child of any age, as if that string has been cut.

It is a terrifying feeling.

You will want to address this issue as honestly and reassuringly as you can. But only after taking a few moments to steady your own nerves. This is going to be a difficult talk to get through. The sample conversation below is cool, calm and rational. It simply represents what you want to cover. You needn't keep your feelings completely in check. In fact, your kids would be very confused if you did. A significant person has, after all, walked out of the house. Your being upset will affirm their emotional reactions and empower your children to face them instead of hide.

"I'm not quite sure where Daddy went. Probably to his office or to a hotel. He's a grown-up and I'm sure he took good care of himself. He needs to sleep just like you and me, and so that's probably where he's gone. He will let us know soon where he is. He's your dad, after all."

Then you will want to address the very sensitive issue concerning *why* he's gone, and communicate your awareness of how upsetting all this is.

"You know, Daddy and I had a big argument about

something. It was a grown-up thing. It had nothing to do with you. Daddy walked out because he was so angry I think he needed to get a little time by himself, away from me. Not you. It's just that we all live together, so in order for him to step away from me he had to leave the house. We'll be fine tonight. I know it doesn't feel good. I feel bad too. But sometimes these things happen. We can talk to Daddy about exactly where he went when he comes home."

The point is to make it clear that this is an issue between you and your husband. He walked out for reasons completely unrelated to your child. And, of course, you must affirm your child's feeling that this is an upsetting event, though Daddy will be okay and that he *will* be back.

Finally, you need to assure your child that this is not, literally, an unspeakable event. Nor will it ever be. You're talking about it now. And you will talk about it once Daddy gets home.

Your twelve-year-old, on the other hand, is likely to have a rough night. He may not speak with you at all about what's happened. Since you may not be clear if your husband will be returning in the middle of the night and your child, by his body language, is making it clear this is not something he wants to discuss, you could make a brief comment before he goes to sleep and then address the issue more directly in the morning. The point is not to push. Don't, fueled by your own anxiety, push your children into talking before they are ready.

"I'm sorry about what's happened tonight. We can talk about it now if you want, or we could wait a bit . . ." It's likely your twelve-year-old will say something like, "It's fine. I'm tired. I'm going to sleep." In this case, let him. He probably needs time to think, feel sad and just kind of live with the event.

In the morning, however, if your husband is not back you will want to address the night's activity a little more directly. But try and be careful about the words you choose. "Daddy walked out," or "Daddy left," can ring the bells of "desertion" and "forever" in a way you will not intend.

"I know you guys know Daddy didn't sleep here last night," is far better, as is, "I think we're all pretty sad Daddy didn't come home last night. You guys might even be angry. I know I am."

Then wait and see what you get. Your seven-year-old may keep at you about when he's coming home. If you don't know you could say so, but with some reassurance tied in. "I'm not sure, but I think he'll call soon and then we'll know." Your older child may stonewall you still, as he is far more aware of the implications of such an event.

He won't want to consciously know much.

It might be a good idea to turn to him and say something like, "Last night was a drag. But Daddy and I got into an argument and he needed some space. It wasn't about you or your brother. He loves you both very much. I think we'll probably be able to understand more together after he gets home, but if you want to talk about it now I'd be happy to see if I can help things."

He might say nothing, or he might try, "What were you fighting about?"

If it's something you can't share, you'll have to get him to respect your privacy in a way that doesn't shut him out. This is a topic we'll cover many times in this book, but for now, simply try, "Well, it was something that's private between Mommy and Daddy. We have very different opinions about something and it got us so angry that Daddy needed to be alone for a while. It's not about you, though, and that's what you have to know. You can't fix what we're angry about, either. Daddy and I will try and work it out when he returns. You can bet on it."

However, if your twelve-year-old continues to build his brick wall in the morning, you can make sure he creates one with plenty of "pass throughs" by simply saying, "That was really upsetting last night. If you want to talk about it with me I'm open. Sometimes talking can make a person feel better."

And then just drop it.

In all likelihood, when your husband comes home your older son will be more able to ask and listen.

◑

Your household has always been one in which people do not easily share their feelings. Things have always been quiet. Unhappiness or dissatisfaction has traditionally been hidden or buried. But now you and your husband have decided on a partial separation. At least for a while. He will be moving out during the week and coming home on weekends, and you have to find a way to discuss this change with your children.

First of all, keep in mind that while your children may not have been able to put clear words or thoughts to their feelings and intuition, chances are they have sensed a change in the atmosphere at home. Perhaps you and your husband no longer engage in light conversation during dinner, whereas before there was some banter at mealtime. He may go out for long walks now, whereas before you would sit and listen to Chopin together.

No matter how small the change, children usually sense a difference.

This does not mean, however, that they are expecting a separation announcement. But you need to keep in mind that children "know" things and need to be respected for their ability to do so. Validating what they experience can only help them gain confidence in their ability to assess the world around them. And remembering that they sense things will help to keep you honest. Your explanations will be truthful rather than reflex reactions offering them only the barest facts.

Of course, talking openly about a very painful situation is bound to be difficult for you. It's hard enough in a family that has been able to openly share troubling feelings. It may feel close to impossible if this is something you've never done. Though this is a decision you can put off until later, it may be necessary to speak to a professional in order to help open up the lines of communication. You might try going as a family so that you can each feel safe and guided as you navigate through a difficult time, or as a couple to discuss ways in which to talk to your children.

In the meantime, since you will want to get things started on your own, it may be best to begin with some honest talk about your family.

"Your dad and I have never found it all that easy to talk about very emotional things, and I'm afraid we haven't helped you kids to do any better. But some-times, even if you're not real comfortable talking about very personal things, they have to get talked about any-way. Daddy and I have to discuss something with you that's going to affect all of us, and it's not a happy thing. In fact, I think we are all going to feel sad or angry. But we will get through it. And if we need help maybe we'll go talk to someone who can help us all."

By beginning in this fashion, you will be pointing out how *each* of you is vulnerable, how each of you has feel-ings you hide and how each of you will share in what's to come. In a way, ironically, you will be drawing your-selves closer as a family. It's possible that through this separation experience, the sharing of the pain will help bring the marriage together. Or, at the very least, it will give the family members a new kind of understanding that will make the connections between them healthier than they were before.

Next, you should lay the facts out on the table. "Daddy and I have not been feeling very good together and think that we need to get some space from each other for a while. We're thinking it will help us under-stand why we are feeling this way and why we're not getting along very well. We hope we can work things out. We will certainly try."

At this point your kids may bombard you with ques-tions, and if you are indeed a family that likes to keep things under control, you may find their obvious fright or distress alarming. As much as possible, try not to shut them out by saying such things as, "There's really noth-ing else to say," or "Everything will be okay," or "Don't be upset."

There is a lot to say along the lines of what it will be like at home. Will routines change? Will you and your husband keep your children informed?

Everything is not okay. Your children know that. To say otherwise is to throw all of you back into a world where bad things have to be hidden, no matter what the price.

And your children have every right to be upset, even if you really do believe your problems will be worked out. Certainly you can say, "Daddy and I want to fix our problems. I hope we can. You should know that." These words will give your children the hope you would like all of you to have, without asking the impossible of them. To be happy. You might also add that your goal is for everyone's life to be as comfortable, warm and happy as possible.

The most important thing to keep in mind is your own limitations in dealing with a troubled marriage in the context of your family. If, as a family, you are not good at facing your feelings, it is extremely important to see a professional who can help everyone look at the truth, in as unthreatening a way as possible.

In the long run, hiding will cause more pain than any amount of direct emotional confrontation ever could. And if you give your children the space to express themselves, their openness may help you to do the same.

◐

You and your husband are fighting constantly. He has been mistreating you terribly in front of your children and you are well aware that things are coming to a head. It's clear the two of you need help. Suddenly your ten-year-old son confronts you tearfully. "Why don't you guys just get a divorce?!"

Hidden questions:

• *Do I have to live with this mess forever?*
• *I'm desperate for all this to stop. Doesn't that matter?*
• *Can't you guys fix this mess?*

The first and most important thing you have to realize about the above question is that it's not necessarily a request that you and your husband actually get a divorce. In fact, as you can see by the last hidden question, it may be just the opposite—a heartfelt scream for you to stay together but without the anger and hurt.

The other critical thing to remember is that you must not make your child feel as if his comment will have any impact on what you eventually do. It's too big a responsibility for him to bear, and if he suspects he could actually influence you, it will leave him feeling frightened, overwhelmed with guilt and depressed. It might even influence his ability to make decisions later on.

The most constructive way to answer this question, coming from any child aged five (she might say "You need another Daddy") to twelve is to address the feeling. "I know what you mean. All this fighting is very difficult. Daddy has been losing his temper a lot and acting in ways that hurt. I probably have too. I don't like it either."

In this way, you will be letting your child know that

he has simply voiced what you already know and feel. He is relieved of responsibility. You will also be affirming his observations, which can go a long way towards giving him a good sense of himself and his ability to see things as they are.

You also need to be direct about his need to know that you care for him in a way that includes protecting him from the emotional or physical violence that he is witnessing. Be direct and in control. You want him to know you are putting together or about to put together a plan to help things.

"It must hurt you a lot to see all this. You shouldn't have to be living with this trouble. Honestly, none of us should, and your dad and I are going to try to do something about it. We're going to talk to someone who can help. Someone whose work it is to help married people with their problems."

There are instances, of course, when a child actually experiences a good deal of relief at the idea that his parents are separating. If there is constant, unbearable tension, or violence of any kind, most children yearn for peace. Even if it means having a parent leave.

The problem is, once the parent is gone, the child must contend with the enormous change, while feeling guilty that he wished the family apart. He may even, once the separation occurs, almost instantaneously wish the parents back together again, terrified of what his wishes have wrought or about what he is now up against. This is why you must be clear that the decision is yours. Your child has to be free of guilt so that he can feel sad. He can recover from that. Guilt is a far more tenacious and destructive emotion.

The Dark Days Before the Break

Children who beg their parents to get a divorce are, unless they are being seriously mistreated, really begging to be taken care of. To be spared the anguish of witnessing such terrible anger. They are trying to bring some order into their own lives by taking the responsibility for a decision on themselves. And, most of all, they are begging to live in a home that feels loving.

◑

You've told your five-year-old daughter that you and your wife will be getting a divorce, but you have not yet left the house. It will, for a number of reasons, take a little while for you to leave, and though your parting is somewhat amicable, there is strain in the air. Also, you sense hope in your daughter. This morning at the breakfast table, sitting between the two of you, she stretched out both her hands, grabbing yours in one and your wife's in the other as if to form an unbreakable chain.

This situation could just as easily have found its way into the next chapter, but it is here for a particular reason.

The child in this case still, in her opinion, has concrete reasons to believe what she wants. The two of you are still together. She doesn't want to acknowledge what she knows, and sees only what she chooses to see.

This is a cruel situation, but unfortunately it's one that exists in many families. Financial issues are such that a quick sale or the upkeep of two places is simply impossible.

The biggest mistake a parent can make in such a case, no matter what the age of the child, is to assume that one conversation about what is happening between the parents will suffice. In most cases it will not.

The child continues to hope things will change, even after a parent has moved out. Certainly, if the two adults are still together, she is even less likely to give up the dream of an end to this "divorce stuff."

You need to remind her gently but consistently of the truth, recognizing how difficult and confusing the picture seems to be.

"Honey, we think you're trying to tell us you wish we didn't have to separate like this. It must be confusing watching us live together. Still, what we told you is true. We are going to be living in different places soon. But we'll always be your mom and dad and you will always be our daughter, and we will always love you more than anything."

A gentle but firm reiteration of the facts will keep her head and heart where they need to be. She will deal with things in good time, in her own way.

◖

Living with uncertainty is difficult for anyone. Sometimes you will be able to answer questions, sometimes you won't. Responses such as "I really don't know," or "I'm just not sure," may leap from your lips many times. If they do, try to accompany them with a soft smile or an affectionate hug. Not a sigh of dejectedness or defeat. Your children will be able to accept that you don't know something. But if you show signs of excessive fear or insecurity you might frighten them unnecessarily and unfairly.

You're entitled to your feelings. Your children can even know that you are sad and sometimes angry. But they also need to know that, while ultimately you are in control, you are not omnipotent. There are things about the future you will all have to find out together.

Contemplating a divorce can be debilitating. Indecision almost always is.

But your children are not the ones required to make the decision. And they will need all their strength to get through this time. Don't debilitate them with your indecision.

By matter-of-factly encouraging talk, by answering what you can in a warm and receptive way, you will give them the sense that whatever happens, everyone will do okay.

6.

As the Separation Takes Place

You've told your child the two of you are separating. You may have to add that a divorce is inevitable or that what happens next is very uncertain. You may be able to speak in hopeful tones about a future of togetherness, or you may not be able to summon a positive note at all. You may keep a stiff upper lip as you lay out the facts to your child, or you may allow a few tears to trickle down your cheeks.

It almost doesn't matter.

Your child is going to be dealing with a set of circumstances that "presentation" will only minimally affect. Depending on the situation, this is what he will see.

• A parent has suddenly, and without warning, *walked out.*

• After much fighting, and terrible tension, one parent is *leaving.*

• With little warning, one parent is *packing.*

• Two parents, after explaining that they will be getting a divorce, remain for financial reasons temporarily in the same house but do not speak, and lead separate lives. They are *rarely home* at the same time during waking hours.

Bottom line? No soft words, encouraging smiles, matter-of-fact tones, tearful explanations, calm or tension-filled discussions will change your child's fundamental observation.

One parent is *gone.*

He is going to feel shocked (even if he's been warned), frightened, lonely, deserted, worried and angry. Even if he's relieved, even if the temperature in the house has been too hot to take, and even if he sees the departing parent often, he will still, for a period of time, feel unhappy and frightened.

And he will be filled with questions, both expressed and unexpressed, that will need swift and direct attention.

In order to address these questions, you will need to have some realistic expectations of yourself as well as your children.

Give Yourself a Break

You have a right to feel anything from traumatized (if the separation is a complete surprise) to very shaky and upset. You also have the right to allow these feelings some outward expression. As we've discussed earlier, trying to bottle them up completely, in the name of protecting your children, could be damaging—for two reasons.

One, it's impossible to ignore your feelings completely. Your unhappiness is bound to find an outlet in other forms, such as unusual preoccupation or temper flare-ups over innocuous events. As a result of your unpredictability and "absence," your children will feel more lonely and confused.

Two, pretending that what's happened is not a cause for sadness would be denying reality. As discussed earlier, children suffer when they are told that what they know is not so. They fail to develop a sense of trust in their own instincts and can suffer from self-esteem problems the rest of their lives.

You have no choice but to convey your confidence in your own and your children's ability to cope. But moderation is key. Your children need to feel that you are in control.

Control does not preclude tears or an impatient word or even an angry remark. And if you make this clear through words and deeds, your children will know it. In fact, they will benefit from your willingness to openly express your feelings.

Even if you are the parent who wanted out and did the leaving, you are entitled to let your children see the departure was painful for you. They may be a little confused, but a simple explanation can clarify things. "I felt that Mommy and I were not very happy anymore and I had to leave. But I still care about her, and not living with you anymore hurts me terribly. So even though I felt I had to do what I did, I feel sad anyway."

As for your children, be prepared for all manner of

acting out: misbehavior at school, unusually rude responses, slammed doors, bed-wetting in young children, fitful sleeping in older children and, perhaps most difficult of all, the "too good child."

The Too Good Child

A child who claims to "understand" may be understanding the wrong thing. "If I'm good this will go away." A child who comes home from school upset, proclaiming, "It's not about you and Daddy," may, in fact, be lying to everyone. Most of all to himself. A child overheard chatting with friends about the divorce as casually as a discussion about the day's homework—"Oh yes. Daddy moved out. But it's cool."—may not be expressing acceptance at all, but rather a desperate need for understanding and empathy.

During this new and stressful period, realize that you should bring your whole self to the task of helping your child. It will be easier for you to speak empathetically if you can admit to your own feelings, and it will be easier for your child to admit to his own knowing you are there, sharing in the difficult experience.

The Questions

You've finished explaining, yet again, how you and your husband have some problems you simply can't resolve. Your nine-year-old son looks you in the eye and exclaims, "But why can't you just forget about them? Maybe it's nobody's fault."

Hidden questions:

The Questions

- *Why can't we go back to normal?*
- *If I do something bad will we split too?*
- *Someone did something awful. But who? Me?*

A child who is desperate for you to "forgive" each other is really begging for life to return to normal. He wants everyone to just apologize, kiss and make up. He is probably terrified to learn that people who have loved each other could actually have to leave each other because of "problems."

It is likely that up until this point your child's contact with problems between people has followed a predictable course. People fight, maybe someone gets punished, certainly people apologize, and then things get back to normal either immediately or very shortly thereafter. This separation is a terrifying departure from the formula.

And one that, especially in younger children, shakes up their concept of unconditional love (though of course they don't label it as such.) They believe that Mommy and Daddy will simply love them no matter what. (All kids worry just a little, at some moments, that their parents will stop loving them.) But many children, especially younger ones, also assume this "everlasting" quality of love is something that exists between their parents. So when that love turns sour, it can seem reasonable to fear they, too, will have to leave when the next problem arises.

The truth is your child, whether he is five or fifteen, needs a matter-of-fact crash course on human relations. There *is* such a thing as irreconcilable differences. For younger children the concept of "problems that wouldn't go away, that kept coming back" will serve the same purpose.

"Daddy and I have had problems for a while. We've tried hard to talk them through and to find ways to make them not appear so often. But we can't. We are just very different people who think about things in very different ways, and that makes it impossible for us to live together. It does happen that people can change over the years in certain ways that make it hard for them to agree on things any longer."

After explaining this you can reassure your child about the way in which the two of you, as parent and child, can work out your disagreements. "You know this has nothing to do with us being able to work out our solutions or look past mistakes you or I make. This is something very particular between husband and wife."

Finally, the issue of who did what to whom and how horrible it was ought to be addressed. Divorce can feel catastrophic to children. A sudden and powerful blow. Many children, in keeping with this feeling, conclude that the cause must have been equally horrific. If they are not busy blaming themselves, then they are busy trying to figure out what terrible thing one or other parent could have done. This is a terrifying thought, because children want to believe their parents incapable of such a monumental misstep.

Ironically, while kids spend a great portion of their day trying to explain to parents how "bad" or "mean" they are, deep in their hearts they have an abiding desire to see their parents as infallible. When they can no longer view them as perfect, it can be frightening.

"I wish Daddy and I could have worked things out, but we're just human beings with lots of complicated feelings and sometimes we can't fix everything. And sometimes we make mistakes. What happened between Daddy and Mommy wasn't one thing. It was a lot of things that built up." At this point it might be useful to draw on an experience your child can understand.

"Remember when you and your friend Billy first had a fight and you were upset but you didn't say anything? Then he did something that upset you again, and then again and again? After a while you just couldn't be friends with Billy anymore. It wasn't that he'd done any one horrible thing. It was just that the two of you weren't connecting well at all. Well, that's how it is with Mommy and Daddy."

And, of course, remember to assure your child that the problems were not about him.

●

Your three-year-old son wakes up in the middle of the night, a month after your husband leaves, crying, "Where's Daddy?! I want Daddy!"

Hidden question:

• *Is Daddy going to disappear?*

As heartbreaking as this very common moment can be, it is important to be as clear and "informative" as you can (and as is appropriate for three in the morning!). Your son is, literally and figuratively, waking up from a nightmare only to find he's actually living one.

He needs comforting and facts. What you say will depend on the particulars of the situation. Has he been to his father's new home yet? If so, remind him. If not, assure him that as soon as his father is settled he'll see his house. Gently suggest he can call his dad first thing in the morning.

In other words, being careful to set up realistic expectations, be as concrete as possible as to where his father is and when he will talk to or see him again. Make it clear his father *exists.* He's out there.

"Daddy isn't sleeping here anymore. But he lives in that apartment with the big tree in front of it that you saw the other day. The name of the street is Elmwood. Daddy loves you very much and he will come here to see you soon, and you'll go there to see him. Now get some sleep and in the morning we'll give Daddy a call. I love you very much."

Sit with him a little while to underline the notion that he is not alone, and then try and leave his room.

The temptation at the sight of such a stressed and innocent child might be to shovel assurances upon him. "Daddy is fine. We'll tell Daddy to come see you tomorrow. You'll see him whenever you want. Everything is fine. Don't worry about anything. Daddy will always be here." A bit of this is fine, but keep in mind that even your three-year-old knows there's big trouble in River City. Giving him a real sense of where his father is—that he's still out there, that he hasn't disappeared, that he can be contacted and that he is still in all of your lives—will reassure your son much more than, "Don't worry, everything will be just fine."

Nothing, right now, is fine. Your child knows that.

What he wants is to reach out and touch someone. His father.

By telling him where he can be found, you will be bringing his father onto the planet and into the town, block and house your child can see or imagine. Young children have trouble with object constancy. A baby thinks, when he does not see something, that it is simply gone. Forever. Your three-year-old has traces of that left. He is afraid that his father is simply gone.

Even a street name can bring his father back into his life.

◐

You have just told your young daughter that you will be getting a divorce. Her reaction is instantaneous, partly, you suspect, because she knew this was coming. "Why did you have me then?!" she cries out with a mixture of anger and upset.

Hidden questions:

- *Do you wish you didn't?*
- *Do you want us to break up too?*

While this kind of heartfelt question can stun you into silence, it is actually one that allows you to give an almost joyous response. So take advantage of it. Your child could use hearing that she *is* the good news. Depending on the age of your child, she will have a greater or lesser awareness of the financial and emotional burdens of a divorce. Certainly she will have heard either or both of you discussing how things will be resolved.

A child can easily take away from these conversations the sense that she is a burden. That it would be easier if she wasn't around. That if you could, you'd wish her away.

"We wanted you very much. You are the biggest reason that Mommy and I feel it was good that we got married! Even though we're not going to be together anymore, both of us feel that you are the happiest thing that's ever happened to us, and so we are grateful that we did get married! Otherwise you wouldn't be here! We will always love you and be your parents. Mommy and I are divorcing each other, but we are sticking with you like glue."

Then it might be wise to address the many problems that concern your child in the divorce. "I know you must hear Daddy and Mommy talking a lot about how we're going to manage, who is going to take care of you when, and other things as well. We are just trying to work out the best way to keep everyone's life going as smoothly as possible. It's not that easy. But we certainly would prefer these complications to not having you. You make the complications totally worth it!"

The magnitude of parental love is incomprehensible to a child.

But that doesn't mean you shouldn't try and explain it. Just try and use words that your child might use to describe her own pleasurable feelings or experiences. That she makes you "happy," that she is the "best" thing that ever happened to you, are concepts she can grasp.

Your eight-year-old boy, upon hearing that his father is going to be getting his own place, at least for a while, cries out, "But I want to live with him! Why can't I?"

Hidden questions:

- *Doesn't he want me?*
- *I'm afraid to live here without him. What will it be like?*
- *Don't I have any say in anything?*

Your child is, first and foremost, desperate to believe he has not been "left." Too, he does not want to feel like a chess piece. He wants to believe that somewhere in this mess he can exercise some control. That his wishes will be addressed. That he won't get lost in the tumult of everyone else's ideas of what he should do and where he should be.

This is quite tricky. The truth is your child does not have much control and you cannot pretend this isn't so. You can, however, help him feel that you hear what he is saying and that you want to help address his needs as he sees them.

If it is a younger child, you need to keep in mind his developmental inability to imagine how a relationship between him and his father could continue if his father is gone. You will want to say something like, "When Daddy is settled, we'll start planning regular time for the two of you to be together. He's *not* disappearing. He's just moving. There's a huge difference."

As for the eight-year-old, you will want to present this in a way that makes it clear this was not a haphazard decision. You and his father discussed, perhaps even argued about, what was best for your son.

"Dad and Mom talked about this issue a lot, and argued too. But finally we agreed you should stay here. We'll work out a schedule that will allow you to see Dad as much as possible, though. We promise you that."

If your child persists in asking "Why," give him honest, practical answers. "Mom is staying either in this house or in this area. You'll be able to be with all your friends and stay in the same school. Dad and I both think it's better for you to have less change. If you went with Dad you might have to go to a new school."

To counteract any hidden fears that your son might have concerning his father not wanting him, you might add, "Dad would have liked you to live with him, but you can't be in two places at the same time. It might seem like it would be fun, but you'd get mixed up and tired and lose things and it could just end up being a mess!"

However, if the truth is your spouse is just as happy not to have the children with him, there's no point lying about it. Your kids are well aware of his degree of involvement (or lack thereof) with them. An out-and-out lie won't wash. But a gentle, comforting, truthful framing of the situation will help a lot. "Dad will not be living in a way that you could be comfortable with him right now. He needs to be living on his own for the time being, but he is just as anxious as you to make a schedule so that he can know when the two of you will be together."

Then encourage your son to speak with his father

about this directly. If your husband is present during this conversation, and depending on his situation, he should be very careful to stress the importance of their relationship and his desire to see his son as much as he can.

"I'm sad (or disappointed) we can't live together right now, but you are my son, and I want to be with you as much as I can. I love you and we will work the times out so that we both know when we can count on seeing each other."

In terms of your son's fear of being at home without his father, especially if there is no other male at home, he could feel thrown back into that old, mostly latent romantic pull towards you. What if his mother expects too much of him? Is he supposed to replace his father? Did he wish his father away so he could be with his mother? And if so, now what?

The most important thing to do is stress that everyone's role will stay the same. In a relaxed and confident manner, simply inform your son that while lots of things are changing, much will stay the same. His room is his. Yours is yours. He's your son, you're his mom, and Penny is his sister. The family is changing because Daddy won't be living here, but you are still you and he is still himself. You don't want anything less or more from him than that.

◑

Your husband, who has just left, is having an affair. Your kids, aged eight and thirteen, sense there is some other important person around and want to know, "Who's Lily?"

Hidden questions:

- *Is she going to be our stepmother?*
- *Is she going to be more important than us?*
- *Is Lily a big secret?*

You must answer this question honestly. Depending on the age of the child, you will need to address it with appropriate information about love and intimacy. Most importantly, it is best not to treat this relationship as one that began with secrecy or dishonesty. This will put your children in the uncomfortable position of feeling as if they have to defend their father, or comfort you—neither of which they should have to do. Rather, concentrate on the reasons for this new relationship.

For a five- through eight-year-old, you will want to say that Lily is a new friend of Daddy's. He likes to talk with her and spend time with her. You could explain, "Daddy and I, as you probably know, just weren't getting along, and it made him terribly unhappy. I think that Lily is someone who helps him feel much better."

Your older child will, of course, understand that this is a much more complex issue. He will know that it involves sex. That your feelings might be hurt. That Lily is, in a way, a replacement for you. That you grow tense sometimes when her name comes up.

Still, try to keep your answers non-accusatory. "I do feel bad about Lily. A little jealous. It hurts that Daddy already has someone new to be with. But I'll get over it and hopefully find someone myself, with whom I can be happier than I was with Daddy. He needed to find someone he could feel comfortable with, and now so do I. This is what happens when people stop giving each other what they need."

If it's clear Lily is a woman your husband was seeing before you split and your children are old enough to know this, don't pretend it isn't so. They need to process these facts. And they need to take their cue from you as to what to do with them—hoping against hope that you will sort them out in a way that feels okay.

"I guess you know Daddy was seeing Lily before I knew about it. That hurt me. I hate that he wasn't telling me the truth. But it happened. I suppose he was confused, didn't want to hurt me and was a little scared himself. That doesn't make it right, and I'm angry about it. But it's done. We have to move on."

Even if you don't feel quite this resolved, you might want to express a perspective that says, "Look, it's bad. But it happened. I don't like it, but there are new things ahead."

Of course, if you're relieved that your soon to be ex has found someone, feel free to say so. "She's a new and good friend of Daddy's and I'm happy for him. It will make him feel good." Saying this will help make it clear that there are still warm feelings between you and your spouse. People can split but still care about each other.

Finally, reassure both children that Lily isn't going to replace anyone. She is a new person in a new position with their father. "Lily is Daddy's new friend, but I am your mother. You may get to know Lily at some point, but still, no matter what, you two are my kids and I'm your mom. Period. The same is true for Daddy. You are his most precious children. Lily can't change that and she can't take your place. Everyone is important in their own way."

●

You and your son have always been very close. You have just told him that you are leaving and now you and his mom are trying to explain to him how the schedule will work. Suddenly he looks up and asks, "Can you and I go out to dinner before you go?"
  Hidden questions:

* *Can we pretend life is normal still?*
* *Are you and I in this together?*

A child who asks a question such as the one above is trying to cement allegiances. "Can we go shopping first?" and "Can we still get those baseball tickets?" are the kinds of questions a kid asks when he wants to be sure you are still a unit.

That you're not leaving your relationship with him.

It's also an attempt to feel aligned—not with the person who seems to be "dumped," but with the one who is taking action. It's a way of trying to feel more in control.

Mom is left behind. I'd better leap to the winning side.

This is just his interpretation of events, born of his need to avoid feeling deserted. And so there's no harm playing along, provided you make it clear that while you intend to stay close with him, this does not necessitate his stepping away from his mother to join "your side."

In the long run, that's neither realistic nor healthy for your son. He needs both relationships and he needs to view both parents as in control and strong.

So be comforting but also firm about the importance of all members of the family.

"Sure. Chinese food for us guys sounds great. And I'll bet you can get Mom to make your favorite ravioli tomorrow," would be just fine. You're happily agreeing to be with him alone, but you're also communicating a respect and support for his relationship with his mother. "Sure, we can go to a baseball game, and when you get back maybe you and Mom can go out and rent a great movie together so you can cool out!"

Your son is also desperately hoping that things can proceed as normal. Certainly you will want to keep things as familiar as possible for him. But it is not a good idea to even imply to him that things will continue as before and that you can all pretend Daddy's absence from the house is really nothing. It isn't. Later on, he will have a horrible sense of betrayal if he realizes you failed to prepare him for the truth.

"You know, going to that Chinese restaurant you like is fun," you might say, "and we'll do that as often as possible when we are together. We'll see how it goes. You know I always love doing things with you. We may even find new things to do when I get settled in my new place."

These are all comments that underline your love for your son as well as your interest in being with him. But they also make it clear that things will be different.

There are some unknowns, and a new kind of "normal" will be taking shape in your lives.

◐

Your twelve-year-old daughter, upon hearing you are getting a divorce, cries out in a state of terrible anxiety, "But what am I going to tell my friends?"
  Hidden questions:

- *Will they reject me?*
- *Do I have to keep this a secret?*

Most adolescents and teens, contrary to popular be-lief, are quite conservative by nature. They want to be accepted. They want things to look right. They don't want to stand out and be noticed for any reason other than to be wholly admired by their peers.

To many kids, divorce can feel like an embarrassing failure in the family. They perceive that the whole world will now know their parents have messed up. And since your child is rooted in this seemingly imperfect unit, she may tend to feel even more flawed than she might ordinarily have. This is a difficult time for fostering self-esteem—even in the best of circumstances.

The first thing you might want to do is point out, mat-ter-of-factly, just how common divorce is. Kids, when overwhelmed by their own problems, often forget to look around and see that they are not alone. (Adults can fall into this trap as well!) You might say, "I know this feels very difficult for you. And maybe even embarrass-ing. But divorce is unfortunately a common occurrence.

It certainly isn't what everyone would wish for, but just because it's happened doesn't mean there's anything to be embarrassed about. You can feel sad, of course. But understand that a divorce only means people can no longer live together happily. It doesn't mean that anyone has done something awful that has to be hidden."

Your child might also be genuinely concerned about what to say to her friends. This is the perfect opportunity for you to explore with your child how helpful it can be to open up to a trusted friend. Talking to a person who really cares can help anyone feel better. You might also want to suggest that there isn't any right or wrong way to describe what's happened. The important thing is to express how you feel to the right people.

"You can tell whatever you want to whomever you think will keep your private thoughts to herself. Talking to a friend could help you sort out how you feel about this divorce. It's important to pick a few friends who can be trusted, so that you don't find your deepest thoughts shared with people who don't know you. It's not that there's any big bad secret about this. It's just that you have a right to your privacy. And don't worry about me. I don't care what you choose to tell. The goal is for you to get things off your chest."

There is, it should be noted, another issue you may have to deal with as a parent. Some kids, of varying age, choose not to discuss the divorce with any friends. They feel too uptight to share anything. You cannot force them to talk, nor should you. But this does not mean that you need to behave as secretively about the divorce around your child and her friends as she might on her own. Clearly, her friends will know what's happening in the house, and to pretend that it isn't will only serve to support your child's feeling that this is, indeed, a terrible secret. If there is occasion in your home when you need to mention something to your child that relates to the divorce, don't hold back because there is company.

For example, if your daughter is making plans with a friend on a day you know she has special plans with her mother, don't pull her aside and furtively whisper, "Aren't you and Mom going to a show?" Rather, say openly, "Oh listen, that's not a good idea. Remember you're seeing *My Fair Lady* with Mom." Just like that. Simple and clean.

Your child will likely tolerate it well and you will be, by your words and actions, underlining the idea that this divorce need not be a state secret.

●

Shortly after getting off the phone with her father, your ten-year-old daughter is quietly sitting in the living room with you. Suddenly she looks at you and says uncertainly, "I know you and Daddy don't like each other much right now, but is it okay with you if I still really love Daddy?"

Hidden questions:

- *Will you punish me for not siding with you?*
- *Will you ask me to leave?*
- *Can we still love each other if I love Daddy?*
- *Is it okay if I sometimes love Daddy more than you?*

Your child may perceive, since you are the parent she

is with the most, that she cannot risk alienating you. You are her best hope for security, and to jeopardize it would be dangerous. On the other hand, the need to love and be loved by her father is equally strong, and so she is thrown into a terrible dilemma.

Is it possible to have both without losing either?

Your answer must be a resounding *"Absolutely."*

"Yes. Not only is it okay, but I want you to love him. It would make me happy. Just because you see us arguing doesn't mean that either of us wants you to feel what we feel. Our problems have nothing to do with you. In fact, if you continue to love Daddy just the way you always have it will be a relief. I don't want you to lose out because of our problems."

You will also want to stress, even in a lighthearted way, that she can have and express all the feelings she has ever had for both of you, whenever she wants. This includes anger, dislike, disappointment and frustration. After all, you are still her parents and she is still your child, and all the feelings she experienced regularly before the divorce must still exist. A divorce can't change that. She might as well let them out!

Children can fear that a divorce changes the rules about feelings. That all bets are off. They can't just feel free to love you a lot one second and hate you the next. Just look at what can happen—people walk out.

"The fact that Daddy and Mommy's feelings have changed for each other does not mean that our feelings for you have changed in any way. Or that yours should change for us. If sometimes you get mad at me and feel like you love Daddy more, that's fine. It's natural. You did that before we separated. Why not now too? So don't worry about it. Having those feelings won't change a thing about what we mean to each other."

The most important issue to communicate to your child is that any feeling is allowed. You don't want her taking sides. She needs to listen to her own heart.

Not yours.

●

Your wife has been experiencing serious emotional problems that have taken a tremendous toll on the marriage and resulted in her leaving rather abruptly. Your children are aware of other separations and divorces, but not one in which the mother has left the house. One evening your ten-year-old, in the presence of his six-year-old sister, blurts out, "How come no one else's mom left?"

Hidden questions:

- *Did we do something especially bad?*
- *Does she want a better family?*

To most children, the mother is the lynchpin of the family. If she leaves it can be an even more devastating blow than the father's departure, for two reasons. One, no matter how strong or weak the relationship between mother and child, there is always the fervent belief in the child's mind that the mother will never leave. Two, since it is common for her to be the more hands-on caretaker, her loss can be frightening. It can also feel humiliating. Especially to an older child.

Yes, it is less common for the mother to leave the

house without the children during a separation or divorce. And since this is a fact, it's one you have to acknowledge to your children. They know it too, and if you don't tell them the truth they will be unable to find solace in any comfort you offer. They will assume your words are false.

"It's true. It's not that common for moms to leave. I imagine it feels especially upsetting. Do people ask you about it?"

Try and find out what your child is up against at school. Unusual circumstances can attract all kinds of difficult questions, and you will want to find out what your child is being asked. Be as empathic as possible, making it clear you think it must be very hard to feel like things are so strange at home and then have to explain them too. Knowing you feel for him will help a lot. You could also offer the following advice for coping with a friend's questions.

• Let your child know he doesn't have to answer any question unless he feels like it. "I'd rather not answer that," is a perfectly fine response.

• Introduce the notion that he can be proud his parents weren't "wishy-washy" about their problems. "Lots of people aren't happy in their marriages. We decided to take a stand. To face how we felt and to try and move on."

Suggest he keep this in mind when answering questions. "My parents," he could say, "realized they had to get on with their lives in a different way."

• Suggest that your child choose very carefully whom he speaks to. Make it clear it's not what he says but whom he says it to that can come back and hurt him. People can be cruel. Tell him to try to choose the friend who is most sympathetic—as well as close-mouthed.

Inform your child that all sorts of unusual things go on in many people's homes. It's just that other people's problems may not be as visible as his are right now. Some parents may sleep in separate rooms. Some may only be home on weekends. This is not to say he should conduct an investigation to see who's got big hidden problems! But it's important that he understand he does not stand alone in unconventional family situations.

Then address the issue of what's happened as honestly as you can. If his mother has been ill and needs help to get better, say so. If you don't know exactly what the family arrangements will be when she gets back, say that too. And whatever you do, make it perfectly clear that her leaving has nothing to do with her love for her children or her satisfaction with them. And that she has left with a good deal of reluctance and sadness.

"Sometimes adults have such big problems that they have to go off on their own and do a lot of work on themselves to feel better. Your mother adores you, but I think she felt she wouldn't be a good mother feeling the way she has been feeling. It made her sad to think that. You can love a person very much but still not be able, for other reasons, to be with them. She and I have had our problems too, and it's not that we didn't care about each other. I know she did not feel she could give you right now what you need. It's sad. But when she's feeling better I think we'll all be able to understand better what happened."

If your younger child still looks dreadfully confused, the only thing you can offer is a lot of hugs and reassurances. "I know this is so hard for you to understand. But I can take care of you. I can't replace Mommy. I know that. But I can love you enough for both of us while she's away. And when she gets back I know you'll feel how much she's missed you and loves you."

If your child tearfully replies, "But what if she never comes back?" and you are sure she will, but not in a shape that might allow her to return to the family or in a way that would make you want to continue the marriage, it's best to be carefully optimistic. Over time you will be able to alter the picture to the developing truth. "You will see Mommy again. I know that. Things may not end up being exactly the same. We might not all be together as we were, but you do have a mommy. She loves you. And she will return so you can see and be with her." You might also talk about the things they will do together when that time comes.

◗

Your ten-year-old son looks you in the eye during one of your first visits with him at your new place and says, "Dad, I don't like it here. I feel funny. I want to go home. Can we go now?"

Hidden questions:

- *If I say I hate this will you guys change your minds?*
- *Exactly how much say do I have?*
- *So how does it feel, me leaving you?*

When a separation first takes place it can feel surreal. Like some perfectly dreadful, dramatic, unreal movie. Most kids would be just as happy to take the script and chuck it.

And if they can't chuck it, they'd like to punish someone for making them play such a key role.

Certainly this kind of behavior is hurtful, and if your son continues to level hostile barbs in your direction you will want to talk to him about it.

But not now. He's letting you know he doesn't like this new arrangement. It doesn't feel right. It doesn't look right. And he wants out. In many ways this is terrific. It's healthy to want to fight what's happened. It's still very early in the process for him and he's not ready to accept it.

Or he may be in the process of accepting it, but still wants to give full expression to his dislike. And to make someone pay for his pain.

You have a choice in this situation. You can certainly take him home. If he looks uncomfortable and unhappy enough, you might want to. He may need to get used to your new digs in small doses until he has adjusted to the facts. But if you do take him home, be sure to be clear about what you expect in the future. "Listen, I'll take you home because I can see you're very uncomfortable. I don't want you to feel that way here or with me. But this is where I live, and I'm going to hope that each time you come, you'll feel a little easier about being here. I love you and there will always be a place for you here."

This brings up an important point. Sometimes in your hurry to find a place you might select one that does not have a clear spot for your child, such as a one-bedroom apartment. Be sure to designate a sleeping area for him and suggest he leave a few things in a dresser to underline your point that he has a place with you.

However, if your son looks more angry than upset, before agreeing to take him home try talking about what's going on in his head. "I'll take you home if that's really what you want, but I think that's not all it is. You look pretty angry to me." And then see what happens. He might take this opportunity to let loose or he might not. If he doesn't, try suggesting an alternative besides returning him to his mother. "Well, if my new place isn't feeling all that comfortable to you right now, why don't we just go out. It isn't time for you to go home and I want to be with you. How about a movie or the park or that new video arcade a few blocks over?" By doing this you will be respecting his wishes, making it clear you want to be with him (which he may be fishing to find out) and illustrating that while he has some control, he doesn't make the rules.

You might comment lightly, as you're walking down the block, "Next time you come over we'll . . ." so that he knows you expect him in your home again. Chances are he'll just nod. Don't expect more. He's getting the picture.

Asking him to like it isn't realistic.

◗◖

When a parent first departs it can be a trauma for everyone, a time filled with anger, sadness, denial and confusion. As much as possible, try to, one, be concrete when you address your children's fears, and two, model honest emotion. Again, moderation is important, but if you allow yourself to express your feelings your children will likely follow suit.

That is the first step to facing the future positively.

The second is making sure, as much as possible, both parents are visible and available.

7

Around, During and Just After the Divorce

Up until now the divorce has not been concrete. It has been a kind of "name without a face." Children know it's something they don't want. That it means both parents will no longer be at home. They know it hurts and that they feel scared.

But what they don't know, what they can't anticipate, are all the far-reaching ramifications of the divorce on their lives. Most parents don't know, either. A divorce is such a dramatic event, it is almost impossible to consider all of the ways it will impact daily life, not to mention special occasions—holidays, vacations and other important events.

Still, adults are able to understand the bigger picture in a way that children cannot. They know that finances will be an issue. They recognize that the dynamics of family events will change. They understand that there will have to be a lot of accommodation in order to make things "work." In this way they are far better prepared for the many unpleasant surprises that may come their way. But they have another advantage as well.

They are not the ones who now have to be shared.

The children are.

During this time, one of the biggest issues your children will have to face is probably that they will have to be "divided up." Both parents want the children in their lives. And, ultimately, the children will benefit from having strong relationships with both parents.

But they will also suffer from the way in which this takes place. Parents who recognize the price the children will pay for having solid relationships with both of them will have a far easier time understanding and helping their children throughout this difficult time. Life's patterns are clearly going to be different. The children will be apprehensive and often angry and resentful.

But you can help them through this time with a lot of patience and respect for their needs, and by being aware of the fact that finding their places in two separate worlds—two separate homes—will be very hard for them. The two worlds have wonderful potential, but that's a revelation your children will come to later. Now is not the time to expect such wisdom.

It Isn't Fair

As stated earlier, your child is now going to be divided. Shared is a nicer word. But torn is sometimes more accurate.

If this sounds a bit cold, it's because at times it may feel that way to your child. Physically and emotionally.

Suddenly he will be told to gather his things. It's time to see Daddy or Mommy. Then, after a while, perhaps just at a moment when he is settling in, he'll be told, again, to get ready, it's time to go. Return to *Start*. Or, at an extended family gathering, he may find himself painfully confronted with just how different things are. Mommy used to go to Grandpa's too. Now she never does. Where is she? What's she doing?

These are not necessarily feelings your child expected to experience. But there they are. He is in a very difficult position and he has to find a way to live with it. This won't be easy. It's a job you can help him with, though, by understanding two things. One, that this is not the life he's used to, that sometimes it feels very unfair and disruptive, and that in many ways it is. Two, that the truth hurts but it must be told. Gently, of course.

In his efforts to sort out what life is now going to be like, your child is likely to ask you many questions— questions that make it clear he doesn't know what to expect and questions that make it clear he doesn't like what's going on at all. There will be challenging questions, nervous questions and poignant questions about very concrete matters. A parent's tendency is often to soft-soap the reply. But try not to. If you and his mother are not going to sit together during your son's concert, say so. Don't offer a "We'll see." Your son will worry and wonder through every note. If he knows you'll be sitting separately, it may briefly sting but then he'll get on with it.

Kids can handle a lot. The truth hurts, but lies often do more damage.

The Questions

It's time for your eight-year-old to leave with his father for the night. But he stages a fit, clinging to his bedpost. He is hysterical. "I don't want to go!" he screams. "Why do I have to go?"

Hidden questions:

- *Doesn't anyone understand I want something else?*
- *Do I always have to do what everyone else says?*
- *Is this, or isn't this, my home?*

The short answer should be that he doesn't.

The long answer is that this is a very complex moment and, depending on the age of the child and general circumstances, should be handled differently.

For the most part, once you and your ex reach a decision about custody and visitation, it should be adhered to. This is so for both of your sakes as well as your child's. Everyone will know the schedule. It may not always feel convenient, but it will foster a predictable pattern. Consistency is one of the most important things a child needs from his parents.

That said, there are endless exceptions.

The child in this situation is clearly very upset. He is a little too young to simply fight you off because "he has other plans." He's not yet a teenager, yearning for independence and anxious to run off with his friends. This is more likely a child who desperately wants, at this moment, not to be uprooted. He needs to be in his primary home—where he feels safe.

You could try and explain that this is certainly his home, but that it is time for him to go with Daddy. "Look, you know this is Daddy's night with you. You'll be back here tomorrow. It must be hard because most of your toys are here, and you sleep here so much more often. This is your main home. I know it's not easy to go back and forth, but this is the way it is now."

But you probably won't get anywhere. Your child is trying to tell you that something about being home now is incredibly important. Perhaps he had a bad day at school or a bad dream the night before. Maybe he just wants to be left alone.

Whatever your child is feeling, he wants you to listen. But you will want to make it clear that though you are open to hearing him, breaking plans cannot become a pattern. There is a fine line between being manipulated and being sensitive, and you will want to tread carefully. "This time you can stay here. You are obviously very upset, and we do not want to hurt you. But we also feel that it's important for you to spend time with each of us, and so next time we'll expect you to do as we've planned." You might also add, so that he feels he has some control, "Maybe for next Sunday we can discuss with you whether Daddy comes early in the morning, or an hour or two later when you've had a chance to play with your toys."

However, if your child is a teenager who is insisting he doesn't want to go, you are going to have to negotiate. He is going through a time in which being with peers is critical to him. It is developmentally appropriate for him to feel this way. It would be unfair and cruel to insist that he divide up his weekends according to a rigid and preset schedule. He needs to be consulted. He should understand that everyone needs time with him, but as his parents you must understand he needs time away from both of you. Parents in intact families constantly complain they never see their teen! It's upsetting but normal. As divorced parents you shouldn't try to sidestep the problem just to stick to your visitation agreement.

Rather, you should find a compromise that is comfortable for everyone.

If your teen insists that a particular weekend isn't going to work for him, don't push. Surprise him with your flexibility, your willingness to bend to his needs. "If you've got something to do that's really important, we'll pick another time. But let's do that now, so it doesn't slip away from us."

In other words, come up with a substitute. It doesn't have to be equal time. But it does have to give both of you an opportunity to be together.

Another approach might be to find a regular time during the weekend which you know will not significantly cut into his time with his friends, such as an early Friday dinner, an early Sunday breakfast or a Saturday late afternoon predinner visit. Make sure he agrees to the schedule and then keep to it.

Despite the way your teen acts, he depends on the certainty that you want to be with him so much.

●

You've just told your ten-year-old daughter that she can't go back to the camp she's been attending. The rea-

son is the money, but you've tried to couch it in other terms. "It's time for a change. You need to broaden out." She listens to you quietly and then blurts out, "But I want to be with my friends! Why can't I?"

Hidden questions:

- *Why is everything changing?*
- *Does this have to do with you and Mommy?*
- *Are you going to take away everything I'm used to?*

Tell her the real reason, gently and with assurances she needs to hear.

Younger children (as opposed to teens) are not quite as panicked about what they can or cannot have, as they are by the fantasy of being poor. They carry it to an extreme. Maybe they'll be out on the street with no clothes, no bed, no toys?

They will, of course, not be happy about having to give up certain luxuries, but as long as you find something to take their place, they will accommodate themselves with a minimum of pain.

"The truth is that because of this divorce and Daddy and Mommy living in separate places, the way in which we spend money is going to have to change a little. We have enough for really important things. You'll always have a home and plenty of food and your toys and clothes. But we are going to have to be careful about other things. Especially the things that we used to do one way but that we could do a little differently and less expensively in another way. Camp is one of those things. You know several children who go to different camps from the one you've been attending. Probably it's because those camps cost a little less. Well, we have to start thinking that way as well."

The point is, don't be afraid to discuss money matters with your child when the subject comes up. The more you tap-dance around the truth, the more she will fantasize about the real reason she can't go to camp. Maybe you don't care about her. Slowly but surely you're going to take away everything that matters. Or, if she suspects this is about money, she may think this is the beginning of the end. Next you'll be telling her you have to live on the streets . . . like those homeless people for whom her class is continually collecting food.

Your teen, however, may have another reaction. If she is used to spending her summer in a particular way, or if all her friends are going on a tour that you cannot afford, she may become angry. It's not that she's spoiled. It's just that she doesn't want this divorce to ruin anything more than it already has. She doesn't want to have to explain things to her friends. She doesn't want to lose status.

What you will want to convey is that you understand these changes are important and scary to her and that you will try to keep them to a minimum. You do have some control over this. *Everything* is not going to be straight downhill from now on.

"I know you're scared. Some things will change, but a lot won't. Maybe you can go to the same camp if we just schedule you there for a briefer time. Or there are fun places to get a job where you can earn some money and hang out with other new kids. Let's be creative and see if we can think of something! Your friends will be your friends, whether they see you every day or not."

It's easy to forget, when steeped in loss and fear, that

distance won't destroy friendship. And that not everyone does everything together. You will want to remind
your child about the other kids she knows who spend
summers at different places all the time. Relationships
survive, and sometimes even grow more precious, with
distance.

There's nothing wrong with a child learning that
money is not a constant. That sometimes one might have
less than others and that it has to be used carefully. This
is the calm message you want to get across. Whatever
you do, try to avoid communicating your deeper long-
term concerns. Your child does not have to know you're
unclear about how to pay for college, or even whether or
not she can continue her tennis lessons. Worry will only
make the issue bigger in her mind. And when you do
have to inform her that something has to be different, try
to present the problem along with a possible solution.
"We may need to look into a scholarship or work program in order to send you to that college," or "Tim, your
tennis instructor is a little expensive for us right now.
But I found a great group class program at the sports
center and I think maybe we should go check it out."

If you keep your tone matter-of-fact but upbeat, as if to
say, "This isn't going to work, but I know we'll find
something that will," then your child will most likely
play along.

◗

*There's no way around it. You have to move. Your chil-
dren were brought up in the house, however, and so
when you tell them, your fourteen-year-old son promptly*

cries out with desperation, "Where are we going to go?" while your seven-year-old daughter softly responds, "But this is my room. How can you make me do this?"

Hidden questions:

• *How can you take away something that means so much to me?*

• *What other horrible things are going to happen now?*

• *Am I going to have to make a whole new life? It feels like I'm losing everything!*

Children of all ages are capable of very strong attachments. In fact, they are capable of investing inanimate objects such as their wallpaper or window seat with such extraordinary meaning that to be separated from them is not just sad but also frightening. Then, too, there are all the factors beyond the walls of a home that concern children. They'll miss their block where they learned to ride a bike, or their friends next door whose home they've always run in and out of with abandon.

What will life be like without these comforting and reassuring sights and people? Life is changing enough with the divorce. Does every other familiar thing have to disappear as well?

To deal with this situation, you need to get some perspective. The simple fact is that moving, in many ways, is a "violent" act, even under the best of circumstances. It is also, in the context of a divorce, a concrete representation of loss. A home is a sanctuary, and even if it's a tense or unhappy one, it's still where everyone knows they "belong." But that sense of belonging comes over time. It's something you develop as you grow more attached to your surroundings. And thus it's hard for children to imagine how it could happen again. This is so even if the family is intact. Their new block and new house and new room will just seem like a place, not like a home.

The move will likely scare and upset them. Especially given the backdrop. Your children might feel as if you are trying to get them to forget their past life altogether!

There is no easy answer to this problem. Words will do very little to comfort. A little extra action, however, will help a lot.

Try to express your understanding and reassure your children that they will grow comfortable with their new surroundings in time. Introduce the possibility of it being an adventure, that there could be some delightful surprises ahead. But do so with a light hand as they are not likely to believe you immediately. It is best, at first, to concentrate on respecting their feelings about their home and the life they had there. Plan some ways that they can stay connected to the most important aspects of their old home. You could suggest a sleepover with certain neighborhood friends, you might help create a scrapbook that commemorates certain parts of the house, including family photos, or you could invite your children's friends to help decorate their new room, etc. The goal is to integrate not just the house, but the experiences in that house. You will want to help your children see that there are ways to bring along much loved and lifelong attachments, no matter where one goes. This is as true for a favorite poster or a memento of a family trip, as it is for a friend. This message extends in a far deeper sense to the parent the children see less often. He or she will always be a part of your children's lives too.

"Just because we're moving to another part of town doesn't mean you have to leave behind the things you care about. We need to think of ways to combine. To make sure your favorite friends and good memories mix with the new stuff in your life. You don't have to just leave your old life behind, you know. You're only changing your address. No one is asking you to leave behind the people and things you love. I know things will be different, but you can still keep those things that are important to you. And while that's happening, I am sure new good things will come too."

Be sure to explore the new house with your children as much as possible before the move, so that they can begin to see new possibilities, or even the "perfect" spot for their much-loved memorabilia.

It's foolish to try to convince your children—no matter what their age—that moving is not upsetting. It is. Things get left behind. But it's wise to inform them that moving on promises new things and does not have to mean a total loss of what was. By integrating the two, you will ease the transition for your children. It will help them see that these practical adjustments to a divorce don't have to actually be as radical as they seem at first.

With a little thought and planning, your children can have plenty of time with old neighborhood friends. Favorite posters, throw rugs and banners can bring a touch of the familiar to a new world. The truth is, the divorce is only one part of your children's upset. The pain over moving would exist under any circumstances. You would need to find ways to ease the transition no matter what.

It's an "answer" that words cannot describe. Your children will have to experience it to believe it.

◗

You are tucking your ten-year-old son into bed when suddenly he looks up and asks, "Are you going to get married again?"

Hidden questions:

- *I'm getting used to "us" now. Are things going to change again?*
- *What if I don't like him or he doesn't like me?*
- *Is it going to happen by surprise? Like the divorce?*
- *Am I going to have a real place anywhere?*
- *Will I like having a "man" around the house?*

This is a question that is best answered, first, by a question.

"Would you like that or not?" is a good place to start. Depending on the circumstances of your divorce, it may be difficult to tell what your child is getting at. Certainly when the father has left but is still maintaining a strong relationship with your son, he will be less likely to want another man in the picture. He's too busy missing the presence of his dad in his home. He may still be fantasizing about how great it would be if the two of you could get back together.

This desire for you to stay single is very common, though often not the easiest thing to hear. Still, you want your son to feel free to come right out and state his preference so that it doesn't fester inside of him, causing fear and guilt. And then you'll want to tell him the truth, making it clear that no matter what you do it won't affect your love for him.

You will want to help him understand a few things about love.

"You know, there are different kinds of love. I love you in one way. I love Grandma and Grandpa in another. And I did love Daddy in another way. I need all these kinds of love in my life because it feels good to give and receive the love in different ways. It would be nice for me to find another man with whom I could enjoy spending time. Whom I could love in a special way that has nothing to do with the way I love you. There is *nothing* like the way a mom loves her child. It's too big to describe. And as for the marriage thing, I'm not sure yet. I suppose I would like to find someone to spend my life with at some point. After all, when you get older you'll be moving out! But I promise I would never marry someone who didn't care about you deeply. Because if he didn't care, I couldn't love him enough to marry him."

You might also want to put a time frame on this. Your child is still probably feeling as if the separation and divorce happened "suddenly." One day you sat him down and told him there was a problem. He'd likely been either blind to the problem or determined to ignore it. He may think that you could just as suddenly get married and force him to include a stranger in his life. Someone he doesn't know or may not like.

"If I do marry, it's not going to be now. And you would have plenty of time to get to know him. It's not going to be a sudden thing, so don't worry about that. A divorce is a serious thing. I can't just trade in one person for another. People are too special. They can't be replaced just like that."

However, if your child says, "Yes, I'd like you to get married again," as good as it sounds, don't let out a sigh of relief at his wonderful adjustment. It may, of course, be genuine. He may want a nice solid man around the house. He may crave, depending on his age, a family that has the "normal" construct. Still, you might want to ask, "How come?" At the very least he may reveal something of his inner thoughts, which are important for you to know.

He may be feeling lonely for a male companion. Perhaps his father has not been available enough. He may be feeling that you've been asking him to take on chores that his dad used to do, or that somehow he's been thrown into the role of "man of the house" and doesn't much like it. He may also be reacting like the "too good child." The one who doesn't want to face his pain and wants your approval.

You might, in response, try saying, "Well, it's nice that you'd like me to get married. I might like it too. But I would understand if you weren't so sure. Neither am I! It's hard to think about having a new member of the family. I'm still feeling sad about your dad and I getting divorced. What do you think would be good about it, though?"

Then listen carefully. You may get some very interesting clues as to your child's needs. If you remain open to what he is saying, you may be able to "fix" many of the issues that are troubling him. While it would be nice if your child felt pleased at the thought of your remarrying, you will want to ensure that he is pleased for the right reasons.

He should be pleased at the idea of a new man entering your lives who will bring everyone love and attention. That this new man can do. What he can't do is fix the relationship between your child and ex, or the problems between you and your child, or your child's disappointment and pain over the divorce.

◑

Your thirteen-year-old daughter is in a school concert Friday night. The day before, over dinner, she anxiously asks, "Will you and Mom be there together?" You are both going, but you will not be sitting together, and so you hesitate.

Hidden questions:

- *Can we sometimes pretend to be a family?*
- *Are you going to embarrass me?*

This is a perfect example of how the little things about divorce, the things kids don't anticipate, can suddenly arise with significant bite.

A divorce, while it quickly becomes public in fact, is something that is mostly played out in private. Your children can go for long periods of time without feeling that when they are out and about "it shows."

But then something like the concert occurs. Or a school play or baseball game. She wants you both there and probably, for that moment, to act as if nothing is different. Why?

Because she's afraid of feeling lonely when she sees other people's parents together. She's afraid of what people will say about her "messed-up" family. She won't know who to talk to first, you or her mother, or whether there will even be a moment when the three of you can stand together, in front of everyone, filled with pride. In fact, she is probably terrified this particular scenario will never happen again—anywhere—and the thought fills her with sorrow. She wants to give both of you pleasure and she wants you to give it back.

It would be best if the two of you could sit together. This is your daughter's night and it should not be marred by the sense that the divorce has "center stage." It would be nicer for her to look out and see the two of you together. She will not assume you are back together, but she will feel good that her parents are there for *her*.

However, you may simply not be able to do this. A bitter divorce may forbid this possibility. In this case, you will have to prepare your daughter. No surprises are acceptable. You can either admit to the tension and explain you can't sit together, or be creative (especially if it's a younger child) and come up with another explanation, which in fact may be quite true. In either case, you will also want to assure her that it will work out just fine.

"I have a feeling Mom is going to go with a few of her friends to the concert. I will be there too, but I suspect we'll sit separately. Neither of us can wait to see you! When the concert's over we'll find you, or you find us. Whoever sees you first gets the first hug. We'll all find each other. You wait and see."

Be warm and be honest. Make it clear she will *not* have to choose between the two of you. Keep in mind, however, that it will be important for you and your ex, for your daughter's sake, to greet each other with civility. Remember, there is a degree of embarrassment tied in with one's parents getting divorced. You won't want to make it any worse for her than it already is.

You might want to add that you and her mother will always be her family, and that while the marriage didn't work, being her parents has been great. This will underline for her that while the relationship between you and her mother is difficult, you will all, in some ways, always have a tie because of her. And that you wouldn't have it any other way.

◖

There is a big family wedding coming up on your side of the family. Your seven-year-old daughter excitedly asks, "Is Daddy going too?"
Hidden questions:

- *Is he still part of the rest of the family?*
- *Do we have to leave him out?*
- *Are we going to get left out of stuff too?*

So far, your children have had to deal with your husband leaving the home and no longer being married to you. That relationship, they realize, is over. They haven't in all likelihood, thought through what other relationships might be over too.

An older child or teen will quickly come to understand that your family may not have much to do with your ex. But a younger child will be confused on this point. After all, she's always seen all of you together.

This is also a particularly sensitive issue because your

children already have to deal with the idea that love ends, or people part or at least semi-disappear. Now, you will have to explain that since you and your husband have parted, he is *technically* no longer a member of your family. That these are your relatives and he came to know them through you. But that when divorces happen, those sorts of attachments can melt away. You may not be close with his relatives either.

"Daddy will not be coming because the people who are getting married are from my side of the family. These are the people that I grew up with and Daddy came to know, but only because of me. Now that we are no longer going to be married, you and I will go to family events on my side alone. And when Daddy sees his family, you will go without me. That's just the way things work. It might feel funny at first, but after a while you'll get used to it."

It is however, extremely important that you point out your kids lose no one. "*You,* on the other hand, get to keep everyone, because you are related to my family and Daddy's family and always will be, no matter what. When *you* get married everyone will be there!"

You will also want to be clear that her dad is not suffering, nor is he surprised by this arrangement. "Daddy understands this very well, and it's fine with him. I think he'll probably miss some members of my family, and I wouldn't be surprised if they talk sometimes. But for the most part, he won't be joining us."

◐

Your nine-year-old comes home from school one day, clearly preoccupied and unhappy. After offering him some cookies and milk you sit down with him at the kitchen table and ask what's wrong. At first he denies there is a problem, and then suddenly he blurts out, "Am I going to be sad forever?"

Hidden questions:

- *Will I ever get used to this?*
- *Why can't I get happy?*

Your son is going through what he has to go through. Grief.

It's as important for him to know it's going to end, as it is for him to understand that feeling sad is a necessary part of starting to feel better. This will be a difficult concept for him to grasp, but try anyway. It will at least let him know that you understand his sadness and that he needn't be afraid of it.

And, of course, you will want to answer his question.

"You will not be sad forever. But this is an unhappy time and so it's not surprising that you feel sad. Lots of times when people feel really bad, they can't imagine feeling better. That's natural. But what happens is that as time passes, and we get used to things that have occurred which we don't like, other things start to happen that we do like. Those new things bring a feeling of happiness with them, and the sadness starts to fade. It's always there somewhere, of course. But it won't always be the first thing you think of. Maybe sometimes at night when you're alone and thinking, sad thoughts will come to you. But they will stop being with you every moment, like they are now. I promise you that."

And then be sure to invite him to share his feelings

with you whenever he needs to. Talking about sad or painful feelings always helps.

◐

Your nine-year-old is in the middle of baking a cake with you when he asks, "When are you and Daddy going to be divorced?"

"Soon," you reply, wondering what he's getting at.

"Oh," he says and then hesitates slightly. "Will people come?"

Hidden questions:

- *What exactly is a divorce?*
- *I want to know when it happens. How will I know?*
- *Is this in-between stuff ever going to be over?*
- *I don't know if I'm going to feel better or worse when it's over. What do you think?*

Most younger children don't fully understand what a divorce is. They have only a basic idea of it. The father and mother will no longer live together and no longer be married. But they have no more sense of the legality behind a marriage than they do of a divorce. They just know that getting married is an event. A happy event. Invitations arrive, people buy presents, everyone gets dressed up and then there's a big party.

Boom! People are married.

So, it follows that what it took to put it together might be what it takes to pull it apart. An event.

Something to put closure on the situation.

You will want to try and be as concrete as possible

about the divorce, and, most importantly, make sure your child knows he will be kept informed.

"A divorce is not something people celebrate, because it isn't the happiest thing. It's not an occasion at all, in fact. It's really a piece of paper that gets signed by a judge in a court of law that says Mommy and Daddy are no longer married. Actually, we aren't even there when the judge signs it, but we will be informed when it happens. Would you like us to tell you when it does?"

Your child might nod seriously at this or simply shrug as if it's all rather boring. It's a safe bet, however, that no matter how he reacts, he *will* want to know. It might be a good idea to explore how he thinks he's going to feel when the divorce is final. You can ask him directly or simply make a few comments that express your understanding.

"I think we'll all be a little sad when it's officially over, but probably a little relieved too. Maybe we can all do something nice for ourselves when the divorce papers get signed. Something to help us feel okay. Do you have any ideas?"

If he doesn't, you could suggest a movie or special lunch or dinner, either with or without your ex.

The idea is not to cover up a sad day, which in a way it is. Rather, you could use some special time together to make it clear what the day is not.

It is not "the end" of the connections among all of you.

But it is a new start, a new chapter, in everyone's lives.

8.

Dating in Front of the Children

Watching a mother or father reach out to another adult for love and intimacy is confusing for any child. The reactions can be deep and polarized.

There is something very positive about seeking new loving partnerships. On a gut level your child knows this, probably picking up your lighter mood and recognizing that people need to seek each other out. Fairy tales, movies, family sitcoms and even cartoons are rife with such imagery. Your child has "noticed."

The onset of your dating will signal that life moves on. This can be a positive, albeit frightening, message. What will it bring? Those same fairy tales that tell of everlasting love also speak of deserted children (Hansel and Gretel) and evil stepmothers (Snow White).

It's hard for any child to know what to expect.

The Threat of a New Partner

Children are threatened by a parent's new love interest. This is true no matter what the relationship: daughter and father/mother or son and father/mother. The issues that are stirred, of course, may differ, and the degree of threat is partly governed by the quality of the relationship between parent and child.

But there is always a perceived threat.

"I want you to love me. I want you all to myself." Between any child and parent there is an element of betrayal and divided loyalties that takes center stage. "How could you do this to Daddy?" And behind it all, the most basic questions fueled by fear will play over and over in your child's mind during this difficult time:

- Will I be replaced?
- What if he/she doesn't like me?
- What if I don't like him/her?
- Will my mother/father change/disappear?

Children of all ages fear that this new person will "change everything." And in some ways they could be right. If you decide to marry the family could move, your children's relationship with the other parent could become strained, your children will have to get used to a new dynamic in the new home and they will have to share you in a way in which they are not accustomed.

But, above all else, your children will be worried about this "replacement"—their replacement, their father/mother's replacement, and even "life replacement" meaning new rules, a new home and new relationships.

It is critical for you to convey the notion that people are not replaceable. This includes your ex. While he or she may not hold a special place in your heart any longer, he or she holds a special place in your life history. He or she is not being replaced but rather bid farewell. Your getting a new partner is not so much an effort to replace him or her, but rather simply a chance for you to care and be cared for, once more, in a special way. Every person is different. Every relationship is unique.

But your love for your children is a constant.

You will want them to understand that no date or new romance can ever take the place of the children.

Your Child's Fondest Wish

Before we go any further, there is one thing that you must understand about your child's inner life.

She will forever, in some way, wish that the two of you could get back together.

She may not say it. She may deny it. She may even be glad you divorced, because of the tension in the house. But somewhere, there is a part of every child that wishes her parents could reconcile.

Dating is a definite sign that this might not happen. That you're not wishing for a reconciliation. That you want something and someone else.

But your child's wish for togetherness is sure and deep, and though some children may know intellectually it's not going to happen, the unconscious desire will hold firm. The result?

Anger.

You're ruining things . . . and you need to be, if not punished, at least second-guessed and reprimanded.

So don't be surprised if the tenor of the questions seems to have no regard for your happiness whatsoever.

The Questions

Your nine-year-old son, after listening to a brief phone conversation between you and a person you are seeing, asks somewhat despondently, "Why do you have to date?"

Hidden questions:

- *Aren't I enough?*
- *Are things going to change? I'm just getting used to the new way.*

The child who asks this question is not so much asking why you have to date, as much as, "How come you have to date given that I don't want you to?"

That is not to say he even understands why you have to date. Chances are he doesn't. So it's important to answer the question, first, with a simple explanation and some recognition that it isn't pleasing to him. "I don't exactly *have* to date," you might begin. "I want to."

This is a rather blunt remark, and one that is likely to startle your child just a little bit. But if you say it warmly and with a smile it will help ease his surprise, and with its straightforwardness it will convey a positive, healthy feeling.

"I love you very much. You will always be special to me. But I also need other kinds of relationships in my life. Even though you love me a lot, you need your special friends and so do I. Still, I know it's probably weird for you to watch me see another woman besides Mommy. Is that right? Do you feel funny about it?"

It's important at this stage to try and draw him out. Depending on his age, he is likely to come up with any number of questions. These are detailed in the rest of this chapter.

With every question, keep in mind that your child feels threatened. He feels as if the introduction of someone new means he is losing you.

In a way he's right. Lately he has probably had you to himself. As discussed earlier in the book, this has its pluses and minuses. But now, because he is sensitized to loss he may want to hang on desperately. Help him see that he needn't hang on. That you will always be there.

And that he will lose nothing that is already his.

◑

Your seven-year-old daughter and fourteen-year-old son are about to meet a man you've been dating for a while. You can tell they are quite nervous. Suddenly your daughter blurts out, "What if I don't like Peter?" You can tell her older brother is waiting, tensely, for your reply.

Hidden questions:

- *What if Peter doesn't like me?*
- *Whose side will you be on?*
- *Why are you doing this? I don't need another father.*
- *Can I be honest with you?*

• *What happens if I don't like him?*

Imagine being very close with someone, forming a tight unit, and then having them say, "Guess what? I'm considering letting someone else in. He's bigger and stronger than you are and we will have a certain kind of relationship that you and I can't have. But never you mind. It'll be great."

You would feel betrayed. After all, the two of you had something going. How come you weren't consulted? You would feel scared. This person, by virtue of his size and age, is more powerful than you. What will he do with that power? Will he use it fairly with you? You would feel somewhat cast aside. Wasn't what the two of you had enough? Now you're being told not only is this not so, but there's something that's going to go on between your special person and her new friend which you will never share. If there are disagreements, where will the new friend's loyalties reside?

The question "What if I don't like Peter," while needing a direct answer, is a distillation of a hundred "What ifs . . ." all circulating around the notion of "Where do I stand with you when it comes to him?"

So begin with the apparent question and then quickly move on.

The most comforting (and hopefully honest) answer you can supply is, "You don't have to like Peter immediately. But if he and I continue to see each other, I hope you will grow to like him. Try not to compare him to your dad, whom I know you love. I'm not pushing you to feel one thing or another. I just think that it would be good for both of you to meet Mommy's new friend."

Your children need to know that you are not simply thrusting them into a whole new situation and expecting them to adapt. They have a right to their feelings. Add the idea that you respect their opinions. That what they think, and why they think it, matters to you.

"If you don't like Peter I'd like to know why. I want to know why he troubles you. I think that's important. Maybe it's a misunderstanding, maybe it's something real. We'll see, if you have something to tell me." By making this point, you will be empowering your children.

Then move on to their position vis-a-vis you. "You are my family. What you think about the people I care about will always matter to me. Being your mom is the most important thing in my life, and always will be. I would never be happy doing things together with someone whom you didn't like, or who treated you badly. In fact, if he treated you badly I'd stop liking him! But I have to say, I hope that you will try to see what is good about a person I like, just as I readily like your friends because you do."

This last comment is important, because it relates your point back to your children's lives. You're nice to their friends. Maybe they can give yours a chance as well.

Then, especially for your older child's benefit, you might add, "I hope you guys will give him a chance. It will make Peter feel good, which will make me feel happy. You know, he's going to be very interested in getting along with you. Keep that in mind. Everyone is a little anxious when they meet someone new. Adults and children."

Be sure to make it clear that everyone's feelings matter

in this situation. Theirs, Peter's and yours. Peter isn't all-powerful. He's vulnerable to your children's reactions as well. This will place Peter in a less threatening light. You want your children to know they count. But so do you. And so does Peter. They do not have the power to break you up, because this relationship is your choice. But they have every right to tell you how they feel and to expect that it will matter to you.

◗

You and your girlfriend Jill have been dating for a while, when your eight-year-old daughter, after watching you kiss Jill good-bye, asks, "Don't you ever miss Mommy?"
  Hidden questions:

* *Is it really over?*
* *Does love just end?*
* *I love my mother. How could you forget her?*
* *How could you do this to her?*

Divorce informs children that love does not always last forever. It's not a happy lesson. Recognizing that you no longer love the other parent can be a sad, disturbing and confusing fact for a child. But hopefully by now you have made it clear that the love of a parent for a child is unlike any other. It won't end.

You will want to make it clear to your daughter that though you do not love her mother in the same way you did when the two of you were married, you do still care. It might be tempting to say, "Yes. Sometimes I miss her a lot," or "I still love her. Just differently."

But don't.

You're introducing too many fine lines, opening the door for more intense fantasies about reconciliation. Your child can take the truth, especially if it's presented in a kind and simple way.

"Actually, I do think about Mommy sometimes. We've been through a lot together, not to mention creating you. I'll always feel something special for her. But one of the reasons we've gotten divorced is that we no longer have the same powerful feelings for each other that we used to. And because of that I can start to feel some of those emotions for someone else. I haven't forgotten about Mommy. But she occupies a different place in my life now."

Finally, your child will want to believe you still care about her mother because she does, and because she may believe that her mother would be hurt that you are with someone else. This could be especially true if you have found someone before her mother has, or have left her mother for another. If your ex is in some pain, which your child is aware of, you will want to address that.

"I know that my leaving your mother was painful to her. Actually it hurt me too. People don't just split, even if it's their choice, without having lots of different feelings. Feelings that don't seem to go together. Like sadness and excitement, or anger and love. She and I both know now that we were not making each other happy. I think your mother is going to be fine. She will also meet someone who cares about her and whom she can care for. I'm sure she knows this. But please believe that I do think of her often and that sometimes I miss the good times between us."

◑

*Your wife has left you for another man, and you've be-
gun to notice that every time your children first arrive,
you become short-tempered and irritable. You never say
anything bad about him, but you can't stop imagining
the sort of relationship the children must have with him.
Finally one day your eight-year-old son, clearly upset by
your behavior, asks, "Why are you so angry all the time
when we first come over?"*

Hidden questions:

- *Do you not want me to come anymore?*
- *Did I do something wrong?*

It will be hurtful to your children if the time spent
with you is fraught with confusion and misunderstanding. They love you and need to know you love them.
And they are more capable than you think of handling
the truth. After all, it's a lot better than what they could
be fearing. Discovering that you are worried about losing
them to someone else is a lot sweeter than worrying you
don't want to see them!

Sparing them the depth of your pain, it's perfectly
okay to tell them about your feelings of jealousy or hurt.
It's even okay to admit you fear they will become so
close to him that they will need you less. Allowing them
to see your vulnerability and to comfort you is fine.

However, asking them to "parent" you is wrong. It's
critical to recognize the difference.

Asking them to assure you of their love is appropriate,
as that is something they are capable of. Asking them to

discuss your feeling of depression or the way in which their mother behaves with the new boyfriend is not. Those two issues are beyond their abilities and business.

"I was hurt when Mommy found Sam. On top of that, sometimes I feel bad about the time you spend with him. I'm glad he's nice to you and that you like him, and I think it's good that you can enjoy each other. But I actually get jealous! I'm worried that you won't want to come here that often as you grow closer to him. The thought gets me upset. And then I get irritable, and then I guess I take it out on you. That's wrong, and I'm sorry."

The important thing here is to make sure your children know you want what's best for them but that you're human and have many different feelings about things. You understand that it's good for them to have a positive relationship with their mother's new significant other, but you love them dearly and want to always be close with them in a special way.

Your kids will likely comfort you easily. It's a small job.

Just make sure you keep it that way. Save the deeper pain for a good friend or therapist.

◑

You're in the middle of getting dressed for a new date, when your fourteen-year-old son wanders in. He sits and watches you with a certain ennui and then suddenly asks, "So who is it this time?" Turning to answer, you are surprised to see an expression of disgust on his face.

There are all sorts of theories on the subject of dating in front of the kids. Some say it should be kept private until you meet "the one." It's too confusing otherwise. What if your children grow close to someone you're dating and then you break up? Others say it's important for your kids to see you moving on in life. Let them meet your dates. It's part of your life and they should be included. Your dating life might even inspire them in their own.

The truth is probably somewhere in the middle.

It's not a great idea to wait until Mr. Right comes along to introduce a date to your children. That will be way too shocking, and you will have been "lying" throughout your dating life. Your kids will wonder what's going on when you're not home, and when you do finally arrive at the door with your "intended" they will have had no chance to adapt to the idea, no less the person.

There is something to be said for allowing your children to understand that real life involves men and women enjoying each other's company, even if they aren't married.

However, a never-ending parade can cheapen this fact. It can take a positive aspect of human relationships and turn it into a shopping spree—one that, on the surface, could seem to give the individual very little worth. You, of course, know that a single date or two with one person is the only way for you to find a companion. But your child is likely to see it as an empty, disquieting practice. Who are these people? Do they matter or don't they? Why do you bother spending time with them if you don't like them? If it's not this guy will it be another?

That is, in all likelihood, why there was a look of disgust on your son's face. It might also have been a disguise for fear.

Is this how it works? he might think. Mom just goes from guy to guy? It's just a game? No one cares?

If you have been dating openly and freely and you catch this disdain from your child, you will want to quickly offer him a respectful way to see your behavior.

"I get the feeling you think what I'm doing is kind of ridiculous. A revolving door sort of thing. Well, I admit it looks that way, but since I don't go to a school every day, where there are lots of people to meet all the time, I have to do things another way. In order to meet people I have to arrange a special time to do so, before I know if we're going to get along. I know we've discussed already that I'd like to find someone whom I can enjoy some special time with. This is the only way to do that! If it bothers you, though, I can meet whomever I'm going out with elsewhere."

Then, no matter what he says, do just that. Children and teens have not had the life experience to know the challenge you are up against. They witness scenes through the prism of their own limited history. Younger children may become confused by too many suitors. Should I talk to him? What if I like him? Will I see him again? Older children or teens are likely to be confused as they try to navigate the romantic waters of their own lives. Do I do what Mom does? Try everyone on for size? Go out with everyone? Get to know this person a little and then move on, and on and on?

When it comes to teens, grown-up dating is particularly tricky because in many ways the two of you are doing the same thing. But you're doing it with a different wisdom and different goals and different rules. You know this. He doesn't.

Which is why it may be wise not to expose him to the entire scene. He may take away the wrong lesson, even though your dating life is right for you.

◐

You have just gotten home quite late from a date and your teenage daughter ambles into your room. Watching you undress, she suddenly asks, "So are you sleeping with Jake?"

Hidden questions:

- *Are you doing with Jake what you did with Dad?*
- *If you're doing it can I do it?*
- *How much do you like him? How close are you?*

Again, your teenager may have trouble understanding the difference between you and her. After all, you're doing what she's doing—or thinking about doing. You're looking for love and closeness and excitement. Doesn't that make you, well, equals?

Actually, no.

By virtue of your age, experience, wisdom and huge responsibility for your children, you are far from equals.

Teenagers are notorious for not accepting "Because I'm an adult and you're not" as an explanation for why they can't do the things you do. But that shouldn't stand in the way of your offering it.

"That is my business," you might say calmly and

evenly. "That's an extremely personal question about something you don't need to know about."

She may come back with all sorts of remarks such as, "Well, you always ask me if I'm having sex," or "So why are you always discussing safe sex with me? Isn't that my business?"

You might want to offer the following observation. It's reasonable and accurate. Just don't expect her to like it!

"Certainly sex is a very private business for everyone. You included. But I am your mother, and sex is a new issue for you and these days a dangerous one as well. You haven't had the experience in the world that I have, and so when I ask you questions it is to protect you. When you ask me questions it's because you're curious. That's different."

You might also, to further buttress your case for privacy, make the following point.

"If I were still with your father, you wouldn't be asking me about my sex life. This situation should be no different."

Finally, you will want to address the issue of how you feel about Jake. Your daughter is clearly curious, or maybe even worried or scared. Describing how you feel about a person you are seeing is not a loss of privacy, but actually a way to have a close moment with your teen.

"I care a lot about Jake and I enjoy the feeling of closeness I have when I'm with him. I don't know exactly what's going to happen with our relationship, but he cares about me and I care about him."

You don't want to shut your daughter out of certain aspects of your emotional life. You simply want to tell her what is appropriate for her age and level of under-standing.

Knowing the details of your sex life is not something that will enhance your daughter's development. On the contrary, it could confuse her terribly. Besides, you need to confidently respect your own right to privacy.

So save her from the morass of connecting her sex life to yours. Keep them separate. And try to be a support as she explores or wonders about that area of her own life.

◑

You have begun dating Ken, a man you like very much. You have no idea if you will end up with him in the long run, but it's a good relationship and you want your children to spend some time with him. Having introduced him once before, you tell your ten-year-old son that you'd like him to join you and Ken at the movies. Filled with apparent irritation, he replies, "Why do I have to go? He's your friend, not mine. Are you going to marry him or something?"

Hidden questions:

• Just because you're ready to include someone in our lives, does it mean I have to be too?

• Is this it? Is this what I've been afraid of? Someone who's going to change everything?

Suggesting to your child that he spend some time with a person who seems to be taking his father's place with you is going to be a loaded issue.

What does it mean? he's going to think.

And he'll be right to wonder.

Chances are you've dated other people before. Your son knows it. But now, suddenly, something new has been introduced. You don't think it's enough that *you* like this person. Now you want your son to like him too. To include him.

Slow down, he's probably thinking. Not so fast.

You may not be going fast at all. But your son might think so, merely because the time has come for him to incorporate someone new into his life, and he doesn't like it.

He may also be suffering from an evolved form of stranger anxiety.

He doesn't know who this person is, and in some visceral way he's afraid this stranger is dangerous. That he won't be safe with this person. He feels threatened and anxious.

Who is this man, what does he want, how is he supposed to behave towards him and could this man hurt him in any way? It's one thing to meet him casually. It's another to have to relate to him. Establish . . . something.

So, just as the stranger backs off from the baby to give him some space, you might consider the same tactic.

"Look, I like Ken and I thought it might be fun for all of us to do something together. But you may not be ready now. That's okay. We can do it another time."

Give your son space. But do it in a way that still allows for your expectation that he will at some point join the two of you. You don't want to push him, but you want to make it clear that you are the adult and that the three of you spending time together is something you want. And that it will happen. Period.

Then you can address the marriage issue.

"Ken and I are good friends. We care about each other and that means we care about what's important to the other person. You're my son, you're special to me, and both he and I would like it if you got to know each other. That's it. There's nothing more complicated going on right now. Marriage is not something we're discussing."

Finally, move to your son's unspoken fears. But do so carefully. To mention what he's "afraid of" might simply make him deny it all. "I'm not afraid!" he might insist. "Who said that?" All of his energy will go to fending you off rather than listening.

"Just because Ken is in my life, it doesn't mean everything has to change. It's true he's a new person and I care for him. And I want you to give Ken an opportunity to be with you too. Meeting someone new can bring all sorts of great new things into your life. And you can bring some very interesting things into his."

Putting them on an equal footing might help your son feel less threatened.

Then tell Ken he may have to try extra hard. Things cannot really be equal right now.

9.

As the Years Pass: Communicating "Long-Distance"

Two or perhaps more years have gone by. You may feel fully recovered, somewhat resolved or still off balance. Divorce is an ongoing process. Even if you feel resolved, there are bound to be lingering issues that occasionally make themselves known.

The same is true for your child.

All of these possibilities can make for very difficult communications. The likelihood of both of you occupying the same emotional space at the same time, as you did when the separation first took place, is small. The trick during this time is to communicate "long-distance." You will need to find a way to understand each other, when it might feel as if the two of you are living in separate countries. Your most important job as a parent during this period will be to stay in touch with your child so that you can help him do what he has to do. And that is to move ahead. Whether you are having difficulty doing so or not.

If You're Feeling Good . . .

Most of your disorientation is gone, replaced by fresh patterns, new faces and positive feelings. There has likely been at least a partial resolution of both practical and emotional problems, and you might be planning or already have started a new life with a new partner. While old nagging feelings of sadness, regret or anger might occasionally surface, you are looking forward now.

If You're Feeling Bad . . .

Keep in mind that it is not unusual for it to take up to five years for a person to find his balance after a divorce. Despite new and possibly pleasant patterns, there might still be good and bad days and a general sense that the storm is not over. Even if there is a new person in your life, there may be days during which you feel regretful or sad.

If Your Child Is Feeling Good . . .

He has likely maintained a very solid and communicative relationship with both parents. The transition from an intact family to a divorced one will have been eased by his general sense of being loved and respected, and enabled by his own developmental ability to adapt. The road will not be a smooth one, however. He will be as burdened as any child with the hopes and dreams of a reconciliation, but he will have found a place to put them . . . somewhere between fantasy and reality.

If Your Child Is Having Trouble . . .

You need to move on with your life. Your child will benefit from seeing that you can "walk through a storm" and come out intact.

But he may not be quite as forward-looking or quite as interested in putting aside past pains.

His new life was not his choice, and it bears constant reminders of what he never wanted to lose. While a certain amount of acceptance marks this time, you should not assume that your child is prepared to smoothly move on. This is particularly true of a child who is old enough to have a full memory of what it was like when the family was together. The person you have left behind is someone he probably wants to continue being with.

Your child still has the awesome job of integrating more of his past life into his present than you do. He is struggling to maintain a solid and loving relationship with his father, while at the same time possibly having to integrate your new partner into his life as well. There is a tendency to idealize what was and what could have been—especially when there's a rough moment between you and your child. A fight over a curfew, or your new husband's stand on a particular matter, can easily mushroom into a "You ruined my life! Why should I listen to you!" kind of confrontation. While these words should not be taken literally, they are indeed an indication of one thing. Your child brings with him, through these years, his own confused feelings.

The "Long-Distance" Problem

Up until this point, much of the pain of disorientation has been shared by the two of you. But this is no longer so. If you are feeling better, it is hard to imagine that your child isn't too. It's extremely easy to stop encouraging your child to express negative feelings. Things seem much more settled for you now, and your child too seems calmer. One reason may be that he has made the healthy decision to try to accept what has happened.

That is different from always liking or doing it.

Then there's the possibility that you are still mired in hurt and sadness, but your child has begun to move on. In fact, his most pressing negative feeling might be his concern for you and your apparent unhappiness. Fielding questions from a child who has moved forward, when you are still feeling bogged down, can be a difficult experience. It is all too easy to bring a child down. . . .

There are a number of standard predictable questions that are asked around this time, which we will cover—always from the realistic perspective of two people coming from very different places, trying to stay in touch. But there are other questions your child might ask at this time, which will take an interesting, less obvious form.

As he moves on, certain issues related to interpersonal relationships may be somewhat problematic for him. Questions will arise concerning these conflicts, and it is important to keep in mind the connection between the divorce and these concerns. Reflective remarks, as described in chapter 3, will be effective here, as you attempt to help your child see the effect the divorce might be having on his life.

You and your child are going to need to get on with your lives. And hopefully you will succeed. Some parents have more trouble than others. Some children struggle more than others. Everyone will be bringing with them a certain degree of loss and pain, no matter how "good" it looks. But unlike in the beginning, when everyone was thrown into the same situation together, each person now has to find a way to climb out in his or her own way and time. You can help your child, but you can't do the work for him.

A child who feels encouraged by both parents to move forward, who is secure in their love, and who is given open and honest help in coming to terms with the deeper effects of a divorce, will come to a perspective that is not debilitating but rather empowering. As a parent, you don't have to be feeling the same sadness, pain or happiness as your child in order to help him adapt to the situation.

But you need to know how he feels and what he needs so that you can help him get on with his life.

The Questions

You have had a very difficult time adjusting to the divorce. Though it was finalized a little over two years ago, and you recognize now that you and your husband were wrong for each other, you can't seem to get past the hurt. Your daughter, on the other hand, after a shaky start, is enjoying eighth grade and her friends. One evening she comes downstairs and says, "I feel bad, Mom. You still seem so sad. Should I stay home tomorrow night?"

Hidden questions:

- *Why aren't you feeling better?*
- *Is it okay with you that I'm feeling happier?*
- *Do I have to feel like you for us to stay close? I don't want to lose you.*

She might as well say, "Mom, I feel guilty. Should I join you in your misery?"

And so, of course, the answer has to be, "No. Of course not! Go out and have a good time. I'll be fine."

But don't stop there. It's not enough. You will need to explain how you are feeling to your daughter in a way that informs her of both your basic strength and your absolute joy that she is feeling good.

"I guess you can sense that I'm a little down. This divorce is taking longer for me to get over than I had anticipated. It's hard being single again. And it does still feel sad to me that the marriage is over. But I'm extremely glad that you're feeling better. And I'm proud too. It hasn't been the easiest thing for you to get through. I'll get there. I know that. I'm just struggling a little."

Admitting that the divorce still hurts will not only bring out into the open something that shouldn't feel like a secret, but will also underline the importance of the relationship you had with your daughter's father. This will, in some ways, make your daughter feel good.

It proves that there was indeed something positive between her parents.

Also, letting her know you are impressed with her ability to move on will help rid her of a fantasy she might have had—that you are either jealous of or angry at her for enjoying her life.

"I'm happy that you're having a good time. When you get back I'd love to hear how the party went!"

Expressing your happiness regarding *her* enjoyment of life will let her know that you want to share her news and stay informed. It will help her see that she doesn't have to hide good things. But be careful not to go too far in the other direction. You cannot live through her. It isn't good for you, and it's too much responsibility for her. She needs to gain inspiration from the way you carry on your life. She will still, on many occasions, take her cue from you.

It won't hurt her to know you are still sad.

But it will hurt her to think she has to bring life home to you, and that your hope for recovery is dim. She will have trouble embracing her life if you steadfastly refuse to find yours. Allowing her to understand why you might be blue is one thing. Asking her to go out and live *for* you is entirely different. It will damage her and cheat you out of finding your own personal happiness.

The message must always be that there is life after divorce.

◖◗

You and your ex split with a lot of animosity. You have a new life and are feeling good again. But still, whenever you see your ex there is tremendous tension in the room. You've just come home from a school play with your fourteen-year-old daughter, who, with tear-filled eyes, asks, "Are you guys ever going to get along?"

Hidden questions:

- *Am I always going to have to feel uncomfortable around the two of you?*
- *We were a family. Can't we sometimes still feel like that together?*

The truth may be that you just don't know. Or, maybe you don't expect a truly peaceful time in the near future. In either case, you will want to answer your child from your current perspective, pointing out that the future is hard to guess. (Try to do so without resurrecting any particular circumstance that has clearly not been resolved by you and your ex.)

"You know that when Dad and I got divorced we had many disagreements. After a while we tried to talk them out, but I don't think we've gotten over how angry and hurt each of us felt. I wish we could, but maybe because of our particular personalities or problems we just haven't moved past it completely. I'm sorry about that. For your sake we should try to keep the unpleasantness to a minimum, and I think we do, but I'll talk to Dad and we'll try harder."

When you say this, your child is likely to shrug her shoulders with a mixture of hopelessness and disappointment. She still wants what she can't have—her family back the way it used to be. While you don't feel this way yourself, it's important to acknowledge her feelings in a way that she can accept. Saying, "I know you wish we could all be together again," might embarrass or insult her—as if you're accusing her of wanting some childish fairy tale. As a result, she might deny your words instead of taking comfort from them. But recognizing her feelings on a deeper level will help her feel loved and respected.

"I can easily see why you wish that when we're all together it could be more loving. We were a family not so long ago. But unfortunately you can't dictate feelings. You can't tell a feeling what to be. There is a lot of sadness and hurt between Dad and me. What's most important, though, is that you and your dad are doing fine, and you and I are doing fine. We love you very much."

Clearly, it would be best if you resolved your issues about the divorce with your ex. Doing so would help you and your child tremendously. If you ever decide to seek professional help to accomplish this, you might want to tell her so. This will give your daughter some hope for the future. Many parents who have remained angry at each other end up in counseling in response to their child's troubles. It is wisest, however, to seek help before your child (or you) manifests significant problems.

◗

Your ten-year-old son, who is helping you set the table one evening, asks, "Can I ever go live with Dad if I want to?"

Hidden questions:

- *Is it okay that I miss him a lot and I want to be with him?*
- *Will you feel terrible if I leave?*
- *Would he like me to live with him?*

Questions of custody are very complicated. When this issue takes center stage, emotions run high and everyone, in some way or another, is victimized. Parents are exhausted by the battle, no matter who wins, and the child, even if he is placed with his parent of choice, usually feels torn, unhappy and confused. This is especially true if the issue reaches the courts, which it often does. There the child is forced to answer all kinds of questions from many different professionals and quickly feels confused or guilty about almost anything he says.

But right now, the child asking this question is probably expressing a few things. He misses the parent he's not with, he wants to know if he has a choice, he's wondering if he's even welcome at the other parent's and he's anxious to be able to express a deep and abiding feeling and to know that you can survive it.

When your son reaches the age of fifteen or sixteen, this question will take on new meaning and "authority." At that point he may be expressing a wish to have more time with his father before college. Or he may want to live with a man while he's going through this complicated time in his life. If he is able to articulate these things, you will want to listen and give his thoughts serious consideration. Especially if his father is ready, willing and able. The decision will presumably be made after great deliberation and many discussions among the three of you about such issues as schooling, other siblings, weekends and more.

You may have a teenage child who you sense is harboring a wish to live with his father but cannot bring himself to say so. In this case, it would be wise to bring his thoughts out into the open so that they don't develop into a dark secret. But make it clear that you are not trying to get your child to move out. "I sense that you've been missing Dad and would like to spend more time with him. Do you want to sit down with us and see if we can work something out?" It isn't necessary to refer to it as "living with Dad." Your child may have a lot of ambivalence about this, and could need to take a less dramatic step.

But a younger child's question has to be treated somewhat less concretely, with more attention to the subtle issues. At the heart of his concern is his desire to be equally close to both of you. He lacks the maturity to understand why he has to be in any one place.

Let's assume that yours is a situation in which it's possible for your child to live with his father. The idea deeply upsets you and you're not at all clear how it could be worked out, given school and other logistical problems, but you cannot say it won't happen. What is the safest reply?

One devoid of hurt and confusion.

You cannot allow your distress at the thought of him leaving to invade your answer. The decision is years away, and in the end it has to be what's best for your son, not you or your ex. At this point, what your son needs to know is that he has your support and that you are willing to talk. He knows he's asked a loaded question. Don't complicate matters by encouraging guilt.

Consider starting with the practical issues.

"I'm not sure if you can or not. That's something we'll have to look at when you're a little older. You're close to school here, and you have a schedule of activities that we've worked out. If you were to go live with Dad it would take a lot of planning. We could do that. But it might make things tough. It may be easier to just work out a schedule with Dad where you see him more than you do right now. But we'll see what's happening as you get older."

Then you will want to address the emotional issues.

"I'm glad you brought this up if it's on your mind. I know you must realize I would be sad if you didn't live with me for a time. I'd miss you so much! But what's especially important to me is that you are happy. We can talk about this as you get older, and if it's something very important to you, Dad and I will talk about the possibility. I know he misses you a lot and he'd love to see more of you. The important thing is I know what you're thinking, and I like that. These feelings you have are your absolute right."

It is critical that your child not experience guilt over his love for either parent or his vacillating need to be with one or the other. It is also important that you openly tell him you would miss him and yet, obviously, not be undone by the thought.

If a child younger than ten asks this question, you can simply say that you don't have an answer for him right now because at this point it's best for him to live with you and be near all of his friends and school. You're glad he asked, though. You want to know what's on his mind, and as time goes by you will all try to do what's best for him.

Finally, if your ex is not capable of properly caring for his son, you will have to share this with your ten-year-old. But try to do so in a way that would not require him to defend his father.

"Because Dad travels so much and because he changes jobs a lot, it would be difficult for you to live with him. I don't feel that your needs would be met. He loves you. It has nothing to do with that. It's just that I'm better set up to help keep your life running in an organized way."

Children of a divorce forever feel torn between their two parents, no matter how well things are handled. It is essential that they feel loved and understood and free to express their needs and feelings. Intact families include children who occasionally cry out, "I love Dad more than you!" or "I wish I didn't have to live in the same house as you!" Why shouldn't yours?

◑

You have remarried and started a new family. Your husband has also found a new and happy life. Suddenly your twelve-year-old daughter wanders into your room and asks worriedly, "If anything happened to you, where would I go?"

Hidden questions:

- *Does Dad still want me?*
- *Would I be all alone?*
- *Does the fact that I live with you mean I belong just to you?*

A natural result of feeling torn between two parents is the confused sense of belonging. If I'm here, then maybe I don't belong there. When I'm there, if I wanted to stay could I? This is my home with Mom, and this is my home with Dad, but which is really my home? Do Mom and Dad both want me as much as the other?

Add to this the fact of both parents moving forward in their separate ways, introducing new faces and possibly other children into the picture, and it's easy to see why your child could feel so unsure. Exactly where does she fit?

And does that picture have any flexibility? Any room for her to "step in" off schedule, beyond visitation, and claim a place for herself?

You do not want your child to feel that her life is restricted now. That would be frightening for her. She knows that "things" can happen. She needs to know that there is a safe place for her should life suddenly change again.

You will want to be able to say to your child "Dad would take care of you, of course! He loves you. You're his child no matter whom he marries or what other children he has. You are as important to him as any other member of his family. He would love and care for you."

However, it is possible that there are concerns. Perhaps your ex is not a devoted parent and your child knows this. Or perhaps he has too many problems to be a full-time parent. Chances are, if this is so your child is well aware of the fact. Whatever the issues, you probably have alternate plans. There are relatives you have spoken to who would care for your child. If so, tell her, simply and frankly, where things stand.

"You might go live with Dad. But if that proved not to be a good idea, and this would be a decision made by your father and other responsible adults, then you would go live with Aunt Karen and Uncle Fred. I've known them forever and they would want to do this. They would love you not simply because you are you but also because you're my child, and both facts would make you very special to them. I've talked to them about this and they said, 'Absolutely. We hope it never comes to pass, because we want you to stay well, but if something should happen of course we'd take Sandra! We would love and take care of her always.' "

Be concrete. Your child is worried and needs factual answers. Names and faces will give her a sense of security. Knowing what would happen will help her worry less about a catastrophe.

But worry, she still will.

Children who go through a divorce lose a certain innocence. This is not a bad thing. Many kids who have not faced a serious loss are later knocked completely off their feet when a difficult situation arises. Children who have been through a divorce have navigated a painful time and have discovered that the world doesn't end. That hurtful things can happen and be survived. They have begun to master some critical life skills. However, they may also have a tendency to worry more, wondering what terrible thing will happen next.

You can't erase these worries. You can only hope to infuse your children with optimism as well, so that what they've learned about the pain of life can be turned into wisdom instead of free-floating anxiety.

You and your boyfriend have decided to marry. You have just told your twelve-year-old daughter, who is now eyeing you doubtfully. "Do you think this one will last?"
Hidden questions:

- *Are you going to upset me again?*
- *How can you try this again after what we've been through?*
- *Do you need me to feel great about this?*

Once you've been through a divorce it's hard not to become a cynic.

Still, as an adult you've had enough experience with life to know that bad things happen to good people, that mistakes are made and that you have to make the decision to keep moving forward. You have to keep trying.

Your child, however, may not get this as easily. Marriage doesn't work that well, she's probably thinking. Why put us through this again? Things have gotten more organized now. Why rock the boat? She doesn't yet understand that you can't let yourself be stopped by situations gone bad or by mistakes. You have to pick yourself up, learn what you can, grow and then try again.

You'll have to explain this to her using a light touch and without any expectation that she will "get it" immediately. Hopefully, however, you will start her thinking about one immutable fact of life.

There are no guarantees, despite what one might like to believe. You do your best to make the right choice. That's life.

"I can't promise you this will work. There are things that happen in life that you can't always predict. But you can take a good and wise chance, using all the information you can get, and have some faith in your own ability to read the situation accurately. I believe that this marriage is going to work. I think so because I know what went wrong with Daddy and me, and I believe whatever mistakes were made won't happen again. I've changed, and I've learned, and I think Bill and I are good for each other. I want to try getting married again because even though things went badly in the end for Daddy and me, there was a time when we were happy. When a marriage is good it can feel great. I want to try again. I wouldn't do it if I thought it wasn't going to work. I wouldn't want to hurt you or me again. The divorce was terribly painful for us all."

Your child is likely to feel somewhat relieved that you have thought about what you're doing, and that you believe in it. She will sense your optimism and determination and will learn a lesson from that. Things can go wrong but you can keep learning, hoping and trying; there are reasons to believe life will go well. But in truth, what she really wants to know from you only time will tell.

She will come away from your conversation knowing this, but also perhaps a little less anxious as she struggles to give your next marriage a chance. That is all you should expect.

◗

You've been remarried a few months to a woman whom your daughter seemed to like very much. Your daughter spends two weekends a month with you as well as one night during the week. It started out fine, but now many little arguments and tensions seem to be erupting between your new wife and your daughter. Your honest assessment is that your daughter has grown hostile. Now, suddenly, after a particularly testy exchange, your daughter rushes past you exclaiming, "How could you have married her?"

Hidden questions:

- *Where do I fit in here?*
- *You don't think Mommy is better than her?*
- *Why do I have to share you when I don't see you that often?*
- *She doesn't like me, does she?*

Stepparents add a complication to a child's divorce plate. One thing should be understood at the outset: Whatever a child feels for a stepparent will be loaded with so many emotional issues that no matter how good or kind the person is, it will make little difference. What will count is how the stepparent copes with the roadblocks that are set up by your child.

Ultimately, patience, maturity, honesty, self-assurance and realistic expectations, on the parts of you and your new spouse, will win out. But it won't be easy.

Your child may have a host of reasons for feeling annoyed with your new wife, several of which are beyond her conscious awareness.

- The relationship may be stirring jealousy and resentment. She wants her father. She's had him to herself for a while . . . and now that's over. On some level it's probably a relief. Your daughter knew this day would come. She knows she can't be all things for you and doesn't want that burden. But it's maddening all the same.

• She may resent your new wife on behalf of her mother. She may feel the new stepparent is to blame for the divorce, or that her presence in your life is hurting her mother.

• She may be transferring her anger at you and her mother for divorcing onto your new spouse because it's safer and she is, after all, ruining any dream of reconciliation.

• She may feel guilty about actually liking her, or guilty about being unable or unwilling to give her a chance.

• You may be pushing her too hard to have a "great relationship" with your new wife.

• She may be feeling unloved and unimportant to everyone, including her stepmother who is the easiest person to rage against. She's never counted on her for anything, so the risk in alienating her is small. On the other hand, she may feel terrified that her stepmother doesn't care about her at all and that she will be rejected. Better to do the rejecting first.

• She may actually not feel comfortable with her stepmother. Perhaps she's more formal than her own mother or has a sense of humor she doesn't understand.

Whatever the reason, it is critical to give your child the time and space she needs to work through her feelings. She needs to know that you understand how terribly complicated all this is. But though you should speak with her empathetically, you should also make it clear that this is not a free-for-all. Your daughter will not be expected to put on a show of acceptance and love, but she cannot be allowed to abuse your new spouse either. It would also be wise, whether or not you think this is so, not to make your daughter feel that her troubles with your new wife are completely her own fault. Even if they mostly are, pointing this out won't help.

"I married Alison because I love her. I think she's a terrific person and I want to be with her. But you know what? I realize you didn't marry her! No one is expecting you to love her. Or even to know how to feel about her. Her role in your life is probably a little confusing to you. She's not your mother, but she is my wife. I love her in one way, and I love you in another. I know it would mean a lot to Alison to have a close relationship with you. And I also think it might make you feel good. But these things can't be pushed."

Once you've established that you neither expect nor need them to leap into each other's arms, you will want to communicate the idea that they *both* need to work at it. Taking this approach will keep your child from desperately needing to get you on her side, which would leave you feeling torn and confused. You don't need that. You have to keep a level head in order to help your wife and child find their way. Be careful not to exaggerate your new wife's affection for your daughter in an effort to help her feel secure. Your daughter won't believe it and will find it impossible to trust your take on the entire matter.

"First, you both need to understand each other a little

better and how you fit into each other's lives. That will take some time. You don't know her that well, and she doesn't know you. But in order for the two of you to find out about each other you're going to have to stop arguing. I know Alison thinks you're a smart and good kid, but how can the two of you even start to appreciate each other with these blowups?"

You will also have to talk with your new wife, in a non-accusatory way, to ascertain if there is anything she is doing or saying that could be adding to your daughter's troubles. She may be trying too hard or feeling a bit resentful herself. If she can share these feelings with you openly it will leave all of you ahead in the game.

Finally, you may need to see whether there are communication problems between your ex and your daughter. If possible, talk to your ex to see whether she can help with the problem. Perhaps your daughter is imagining feelings your wife doesn't have, or your ex is communicating thoughts that might better be kept private.

Whatever happens, keep in mind one thing. You can't tell your daughter whom or when to love. You can only set some rules, listen, and help her feel safe enough to be more open to a positive relationship.

Your handsome fifteen-year-old son already has girls chasing after him. You notice, however, that he is exhibiting behavior that is rather out of character. He's always been a serious person who treats his friends and other people with care. But now he seems to take no girl seriously. You lightly comment, "So do you like Emily?"

He rolls his eyes and replies, "Not really. Is that a problem?"

You sense from his tone that maybe it is.

Hidden questions:

- *I don't really like to get close to anyone. Is that okay?*
- *Am I supposed to want a girlfriend?*
- *Something feels scary to me, but what?*
- *Why should I set myself up for being dumped again?*

Children who have gone through a divorce, no matter what their age, can have difficulty with *trust*. They have felt betrayed by the people with whom they had the closest ties. These parent-child relationships are the models upon which future commitments are made, and are therefore an unsteady platform upon which to venture into romance and the attendant intimacy and trust.

It should be kept in mind that there is a level of immaturity in all young teens when it comes to forming relationships with the opposite sex, and so it is dangerous and unfair to blame everything on a divorce. This is a time for exploration. There could be a different girl every month and that might be quite normal.

Still, it is true that many children coming from a divorce have difficulty trusting others enough to invest their feelings in a full and loving way. They may not make this connection, however. Unwilling to revisit their feelings about the divorce, the pain is expressed through their seeming independence. Afraid of getting hurt again, they may shy away from commitment. The more painful the divorce, the more dramatic this problem usually becomes.

It is therefore a good idea to try to help your teen make the connection. But, as usual, you must do so with a very light hand. This isn't Eurekaville. You can't expect him to say, "Oh wow! You mean because I felt so deserted by the two of you, because you both hurt me by getting a divorce, I'm afraid to get real close to anyone! Yeah? Let me call Emily and tell her all about it!"

Your son will need, with some guidance from you, to approach the connection gradually.

Using the reflective techniques discussed earlier in this book, gently try to bring him to the ways in which his social behavior might reflect the divorce experience.

"Do you think it's a problem?" you might first ask. "Do you want to be with a girl who is special to you?"

No matter how he answers, you might try saying, "You know, sometimes certain experiences in people's lives really make them scared about feeling attached to another person. Divorce can make a person feel like they don't want to get too close to anyone again because they might get hurt. That's true for adults and kids."

Let that sit a moment. If your child seems receptive you might want to go just a little further.

"But you know one hurt doesn't necessarily mean another will happen. Every relationship is different. It's important to give people a chance."

And then, unless your son engages you in a full conversation, let it go.

But stay observant. If it appears that he really is having trouble connecting, you might want to get him some help. Many teens are shy about becoming meaningfully involved with another person, but a child who has gone through a divorce might find it particularly difficult.

The longer his reticence continues, the more ingrained it may become and the more healthy growing experiences he could miss.

You will want to step in before it causes him serious trouble during a time when important personal commitments would truly enhance his life and help him mature.

◑

Your daughter came home the other day completely devastated by a breakup with a boyfriend she'd been seeing only two months. She can't stop crying. Finally she turns to you and says, "Mom, why does it hurt so much?"

Breaking up is difficult for any teen. In fact, it's difficult for any adult too. Whether or not a child has been through a divorce, a broken romance can be a blow to her self-esteem. Also, since so many young teens are unfamiliar with the joys and woes of intimacy, they may throw themselves into a relationship with such innocent abandon that when it falls apart they do too—out of shock.

But a child who has gone through a divorce may not be in shock. Rather, she might be tortured by a terrible familiarity. A sense that she's been in this awful spot before and that this feeling of being deserted or rejected is too much to stand again.

She is likely, however, not to realize the deep connection between her feeling of having been "left" by her father and the loss of this boyfriend. You might want to help her see how one hurtful experience can remind her so much of a past, even more serious, one that all the old intense feelings come flooding back. The result is that this new problem feels worse than it is.

Begin by expressing your understanding for the immediate situation. To do otherwise would be to undermine the truly sad experience of any breakup.

"I think it's hard when a romance is over. It's difficult when you've felt close to someone, because when it's over it feels like a loss. And in a way it is. But you gave him something and he gave you something and you'll both always have that. It becomes a part of you. A kind of bittersweet memory. Right now it makes you very sad. But in time part of that memory will fill you with nice feelings."

Then you can move on to helping her make the connection between these facts and the divorce. "But you know sometimes when a person feels really bad about something, it's not just because of the situation in front of them. Sometimes it's because that situation reminds them of something else that hurt, maybe even worse, in the past. You know when Daddy and I split up, it was kind of like we all broke up. That made us all feel terribly sad. Do you think maybe the way you're feeling reminds you of that time?"

She may nod. She may deny it. She may reply defensively that this is all about her and Paul and you just don't understand. But you will still have planted a thought in her head that will likely stick. She can't, of course, be her own analyst. No one can. And she has neither the maturity nor the intellectual sophistication to fully grasp how one event can affect another. But it will be very helpful to her throughout her life to stay aware of the ways the divorce may be impacting her personal life. This awareness, no matter how vague, will help calm her anxieties and propel her into therapy if unhappy patterns persist.

Finally, try to remind your child, when talking about the losses in your lives, that these sorrows are part of your personal life stories. Joy and sorrow are in our hearts always, and that's part of what makes us who we are. These experiences can make us stronger and kinder people.

◐

Every adult deals differently with the first years following a divorce. The path to recovery is bumpier or longer for some than it is for others. The same is true for your child.

Recovery from divorce is a highly disorganized process that could have a few steps forward, a few steps backward and then one more forward again. This unpredictability makes it almost impossible for you and your child to go through this transitional time hand in hand. In fact, it makes it especially difficult to know what is going on with your child. He may be clearly upset or appear resolved, secretly and actively dealing with many difficult feelings. Caught up in your own drama during this time, a gulf could develop between you and your child that places a very unfortunate distance between you.

Remind yourself a divorce is an ongoing event for everyone. This is true no matter how resolved you feel. Keeping this in mind will help you recognize when your

child needs help, and will ultimately help him feel less
alone and far more able to cope with the conflicting feelings that will assail him from time to time.

It will also help you come to terms with your own inner conflicts, which surely exist no matter how well you
have managed to move forward in your life.

10.

Life Questions

Most parents would like their children to retain their innocence as long as possible. There's time enough to discover that things aren't always fair. That bad things happen to good people. And that almost nothing in life is ever problem-free.

Somehow the vision of our children waking up in the morning, filled with happy anticipation, seems right. The way things should be. Never mind that the world is a cruel place, or that deep in the recesses of our children's minds all sorts of anxieties are lurking.

At the conclusion of most fairy tales, our children are told, "They lived happily ever after." And that is what we would like them to believe.

Even after a divorce.

Certainly in the face of such a loss, you do not expect your child to completely embrace the notion of life's happy predictability. Still, the tendency is to hope that, having weathered the bad times, he will emerge smiling, filled with a joyful anticipation of the future.

And maybe he will. Hopefully the divorce will not have stripped your child of his belief that life still holds great promise.

But it is unrealistic to assume that a smile represents a return to basic innocence. That the world once again appears the way it did—a place where disappointments exist, but also where good triumphs over evil cleanly and conclusively. The fairy tales don't examine whether or not Cinderella, having survived a weak father and three cruel stepsisters, was able to face the morning one year later with her self-esteem intact. They don't describe Snow White's attitude towards life after having been a victim of a vicious crime. Or how in the world Hansel and Gretel could ever trust their father again. The tales simply leave children with the notion that, the bad times over and notwithstanding, it's time to let the good times roll.

The stories, in other words, remain unfinished—cut short at the point of adjustment and recovery.

Your child's story, however, will not be that way.

Having survived a divorce, he has lost a large part of his innocence. The best thing you can do now is to recognize and embrace that fact.

It is not bad news. It is opportunity.

It has come perhaps a little earlier than you would have liked, and been inspired by a loss you would have been glad to avoid. But it is a moment that was bound to come.

A divorce will alter your child's perspective on trust, love, family and the concept of permanence. He will, without a doubt, no longer view life as predictable or orderly or something over which he has complete control. He will know that he doesn't deserve some of the things that can happen, and that you are not only imperfect but that you cannot always protect him.

He will view life differently from the way he did before the divorce. He will undoubtedly be filled with deep and sometimes complicated questions.

The challenge to you as a parent will be to help him see things realistically instead of negatively, and to frame events in a way that offers positive possibilities.

The most important thing you can do for your child is to help him develop a healthy, honest perspective on life—one that acknowledges the potential pain but sees hope for happiness, success and love.

When your child asks about life, don't be afraid to bring what you know to the table. It will hurt you both to confirm what your child has already discovered: not everything can be righted in the end. And, yes, it might have been better for your child to keep his innocence a little longer. But the truth is he had to lose it some time.

Besides, you really have no choice but to talk about life with honesty and directness. Your child knows the truth. He just needs you to confirm his perception and help him make sense of it.

The Questions

How come you got a divorce but other people don't?
 Hidden questions:

 • *Why are we different?*

- *What's wrong with us?*
- *Are we the only ones like this in the world?*

No child likes to feel different. Somehow "different" usually means something negative. But what your child needs to understand is that *everyone* is different from everyone else. Also divorce is one solution to a problem that *many* people share. Other people reach other solutions which may be even more painful.

And, finally, that "being married" is not necessarily the norm.

To explain this basic truth you will want to offer some sociological information.

- Approximately 50 percent of all marriages in this country end in divorce.
- There are some places in the world where no one gets married.
- There are other countries where men have several wives.
- Some places in the world don't allow divorce.
- Some societies are organized around extended family groups in which aunts, uncles, cousins, parents, children, grandparents and others all live under the same roof, dividing child-rearing duties.

"So," you might conclude, "what's normal?"

Your child may reply all of this doesn't matter. He lives here, and hardly anyone he knows comes from a divorced home. Everyone's happy. Only his family fell apart.

At this point you may want to talk about the American dream. You shouldn't put it down, but rather describe it as an ideal. Something perfect in concept that isn't always as it appears and very often doesn't exist. Period.

"I know there are lots of shows on TV where there's a Mommy and Daddy and two children. Advertisements show happy families sitting around breakfast tables. But everyone on screen is an actor or actress playing a family as we would like to believe families are. In real life, at least half of those actors come from either divorced homes or homes with lots of problems. Because that's real life. You may look around and see all your friends in homes with everyone still living there, but it may not be as joyous as you think. Remember how you came home last week and said that Peter's dad went in his room and slammed the door? And that he yelled at Peter's mom? Well, sometimes family life is great and sometimes it isn't. Sometimes it works and sometimes it doesn't. And just because things look a certain way doesn't make it so. Our family worked out its problems one way. Others choose another way. In fact, lots of families have problems and can't figure out how to help themselves at all, and so they do nothing. This hurts everyone much more. The bottom line is that there is no right or wrong. There is no one way to do things."

Everybody has a right to reach the decision they think will work best for them. This is a lesson your child would do well to learn.

And teaching him that making things "look good" is not the road to happiness is a lesson of incalculable value.

If you really love someone, how come it doesn't last?
   Hidden questions:

   • *Could you stop loving me?*
   • *Could this happen to you again?*
   • *Could I stop loving someone too?*

The romantic, innocent notion of love is that it lasts forever. It's a powerful thought and almost everyone wants to believe it. Up until the divorce your child, too, probably assumed you and your spouse would love each other permanently. That it was not up for debate.

She's learned otherwise.

But what she doesn't understand is how that can be.

It's a frightening proposition. Does love just . . . well . . . disappear? If a person does something really bad does it just fly out the window?

What makes love "work" or not "work" is a complicated issue and not one your child will be able to fully understand. But you need to communicate the basic facts about how and why love can or cannot last, if just to quell her anxieties. Knowing that love is not a feeling that simply vanishes will help considerably.

Start with you and her. It is critical that your child understand there are different kinds of love (which has been covered earlier in this book) in order for her to really listen to what you have to say about romantic love. Explain that love includes forgiveness and tolerance, so that when she sees you are angry with her, she is clear that this does not negate the love.

"I'm going to answer this question in terms of a love relationship between a man and a woman. This is a different kind of love from what a parent feels for a child. That is a very sure and permanent thing and unlike any other kind of love. We will always be tied to each other in a way that a man and woman are not. Even when I'm angry or upset with you I love you. Those feelings do not erase my love. They are what happens as a part of our relationship."

Once you've explained the difference, it is safe to move to the subject of love's transience.

"Sometimes love does last even though people can't be together anymore. The love is not the same as it was when they got married. Adults who get divorced cannot live together, because they cannot be happy with each other. In a sense they've stopped liking each other. Enjoying each other. To live with each other is too upsetting or angering or disappointing. That tolerance I spoke of, and forgiveness, gets used up after a while in a way it cannot between a parent and child."

Of course, love can die. And since it's true, you will want to say so.

"But sometimes it is true that love goes away. Circumstances and situations arise that make it difficult for love to continue. Other times each person is so distressed by the other that the love is no longer there."

Don't be afraid to be concrete, using an example or two from your own marriage.

"You know that one of the problems between Mommy and me was money. Mommy needed me to work in a particular way so that she could feel secure. I didn't want to do that. I made her unhappy and she made me feel badly too. Then we started arguing a lot, and pretty soon we weren't liking each other very much. We were too angry. But do I still think Mommy has a great sense of humor? Yes. Do I miss her sometimes? Yes. Do I still love her? Probably in a way. But we couldn't live together anymore and the love definitely changed."

It would also be a good idea to bring in the concepts of taking care of oneself and achieving a balance in one's life.

"There are strong and weak aspects to the way everyone gets along with another person. Some people, for example, regularly fight about one person being late or the other hogging the conversation, but get along great when it comes to sharing important feelings. What matters is when the balance tips too much to the difficult side. When the pain starts taking up too much of the relationship and your heart begins to hurt too much, sometimes people have to separate. They need to restore the peace in their hearts."

Finally, you will want to address the notion of how people simply change. Sometimes they can grow together, sometimes they can't. Sometimes people change in ways that make it hard for them to get along.

It might be possible to bring in an example from your child's life. "Remember when in second grade you had a very best friend named Renee? Then by the time the end of third grade rolled around you weren't feeling so close to her anymore. You liked her but Amy seemed to be someone with whom you enjoyed more things. Well, probably you and Renee changed. It doesn't mean your friendship in second grade wasn't real. It was real. But then things happened and you began to need different things that Amy could offer more readily."

You might want to add that children go through all kinds of transformations as they go out into the world, but that the parent-child relationship is different on this score. It isn't necessary for a child to stay the way she has always been or change in a way that seems "right" or "expected" to a parent for them to remain connected. The parent-child relationship does not require the same sort of compatibility that a husband-wife relationship does.

The bottom line is that love doesn't ever suddenly just disappear. Rather, it comes up against obstacles, some of which can be overcome and some not.

◑

Can I ever trust anyone not to hurt me?
   Hidden question:

• *I thought you wouldn't hurt me and you did. If I can't trust you, whom can I trust?*

You made the decision to get the divorce. Not your child. He knows this. He also knows you feel badly about hurting him. But you did anyway. This is difficult to reconcile, given that he believes you love him very much. So it is easy to see why a child would pause and ask, given what you've done, whether there is anyone on earth who wouldn't hurt him.

The answer is no. There is no point hiding from this

fact. But it is critical for you to point out that there are many people who would never do so intentionally. And this includes you. It's simply that sometimes life forces decisions that hurt but which help make things better in the long run.

Point out that human relationships are very difficult. Everyone comes to them with their own different sets of dreams and expectations about the other person. But no one can ever fulfill all of them. This is normal. Sometimes the ability of one person to make another happy grows weaker and weaker. Again, it's a question of people changing. Not betrayal.

"At first Mom and I felt as if we were always there for each other. But then, as time went by and life brought new problems and challenges, it seemed I couldn't be everything your mother needed me to be and she couldn't be everything I needed her to be. As more time passed, we began to feel lonely with each other and ultimately decided we needed to find others with whom we could be happy. This hurt us and it hurt you. We didn't want that. But we earnestly believe that our unhappiness would have made our lives too difficult and would have ultimately hurt you as well."

Perhaps the most gentle way to answer this basic question about trust, then, would be to say, "You can trust people whom you love and who love you enough not to *want* to hurt you. But sometimes they can't help it. And sometimes you will hurt them as well. You can trust in their desire for you to be happy. But you cannot fault them for having their own needs or yourself for looking out for your own."

Your child needs to see that he can trust people, but

that no one is perfect or totally unselfish. He also needs to understand that he should take his time trusting a person. He needs to be sure of the person's integrity and honesty. And that sometimes even if a person is wonderful, she will have a need that sometimes directly conflicts with a need of your child's. It doesn't mean he can't trust this person. It means he has to understand that life often places people in the difficult position of having to make a choice that's going to hurt someone—either way.

Finally, as a parent, understand that you will not, by virtue of the divorce, obliterate your child's trust in you. The critical factor is your ability to remain truthful with him throughout, and to trust that your decision is an act of faith and courage. Your bad news will not be the betrayal. Your inability to face it head-on will.

◑

Why should anyone get married if this can happen?

A child who asks this question is obviously feeling a little cynical. Why, she is asking, set yourself up for a fall?

The reason, of course, is that you hope you won't fall. And that for many people it's worth the chance. People, you should impress upon her, aren't foolish when they give marriage a chance. They are, rather, hopeful and full of dreams—many of which are realistic, some of which are not.

"People get married because it is a comforting, loving and romantic thought. They believe it will be forever.

They are feeling wonderful and 'in love' and are very happy to have this part of their life settled. Also, life can be difficult, and it is nice to have a companion. Certainly everyone knows people get divorced and that this could happen to them, but they are hoping it won't."

Then you might want to back off and speak philosophically about how, if you hide from every important experience because it carries risks, you could have a very uninteresting and unsatisfying life. Besides, even if you try and things don't work out, the results can be survived.

"A divorce is a very sad event. But it doesn't have to ruin anyone's life. It takes a while to feel better, but then other things in life begin to happen and everyone moves on. Certainly they bring the sadness of a lost relationship with them. But they bring something else too. Chances are during the marriage there were many good experiences. Growing experiences. And these experiences travel with people in their hearts forever. A marriage falling apart does not necessarily mean the marriage should never have happened. It just means it lost its goodness and joy."

That is the central message of this book, which you will want to convey to your child. It's an issue of respect. The pain of the divorce deserves it, the needs of everyone involved deserve it and the marriage itself deserves it. In the end, then, the divorce becomes a necessary though difficult passage to something new. It becomes part of everyone's life story. But it does not have to overwhelm, define or destroy it.

A divorce is a loss. But it is also a solution.

As long as you are able to talk about it.

INDEX

Index